·BUILD·IT·BETTER·YOURSELF·
WOODWORKING PROJECTS

Country Furniture

Kitchens and Dining Rooms

Collected and Written
by Nick Engler

Rodale Press
Emmaus, Pennsylvania

Printed in the United States of America

Series Editor: William H. Hylton
Managing Editor/Author: Nick Engler
Copy Editor: Kate Armpriester
Graphic Designer: Linda Watts
Graphic Artist: Linda Ball
Draftspersons: Mary Jane Favorite
              Chris Walendzak
Photography: Karen Callahan
Cover Photography: Mitch Mandel
Illustrations by O'Neil & Associates, Dayton, Ohio
Produced by Bookworks, Inc., West Milton, Ohio

If you have any questions or comments concerning this book, please write:
Rodale Press
Book Reader Service
33 East Minor Street
Emmaus, PA 18098

Library of Congress Cataloging-in-Publication Data

Engler, Nick.
  Country Furniture.

  (Build-it-better-yourself woodworking projects)
  1. Woodwork. 2. Country furniture. I. Title
II. Series.
TS180.E54   1988   684.1'04   88–26445
ISBN 0–87857–790–4 hardcover
ISBN 0–87857–852–8 paperback

Distributed in the book trade by St. Martin's Press

  4 6 8 10 9 7 5 3   hardcover
2 4 6 8 10 9 7 5 3 1   paperback

Contents

The Roots of American Country Furniture

"Yankee ingenuity" was essential if the frontier was to be tamed, if the house was ever to become a home.
— *Jerard Jordan*

Before you begin to build the projects in this book, pause and reflect on this for a moment: "Country" is much more than a style of furniture; it's a rich heritage. The roots of this style stretch back over hundreds of years to the very beginnings of this nation. Each piece, each specific form — the dry sinks, the trestle tables, the ladder-back chairs — played a part in a grand adventure. These were the inventions and innovations of a restless, energetic people — your grandfathers and grandmothers — who, with only the crudest of tools, built a new life for themselves in a wild, dangerous place they called America.

The Beginnings

The first settlers, the transplanted English who arrived in the 1600s, brought with them little of their own furniture. Their ships were no more than twice the size of a three-bedroom house. Crowded with as many as 100 people (the *Mayflower* carried 102) and provisions for the journey, there was scant room for furniture. Instead, the settlers brought with them woodworkers and tools. A peculiar English law, part of the Tunnage Acts, required that a ship return to England with as many wooden casks for food and drink as it set out with. So each of the early American settlements included at least one skilled woodworker to mend the casks or make new ones.

When the woodworkers had finished making casks, they began to build houses and furnish them. (The master woodworker at the Plymouth colony was John Alden, who had come over on the *Mayflower*. Alden became the first furnituremaker in the New World.)

These craftsmen copied the few pieces they had brought with them, or built furniture similar to what they remembered from home. For the most part, these were massive, heavily-constructed chairs, tables, chests, and bedsteads, built in the "Jacobean" style that was popular then in northern Europe. Jacobean furniture was some of the last furniture to be produced in the old medieval tradition of "joyners."

Joyners (or joiners) were general woodworkers; they joined wood. They did not specialize in cabinetry or carpentry; joining (woodworking) was enough of a specialty. If you were a joiner, you made houses when it was warm enough to work outside and furniture when it wasn't. Consequently, much of the furniture that was made by joiners was built like a house, with heavy frame members and large joints.

The settlers found that the style was uniquely suited to their circumstances. Their tools were housebuilding or shipwright's tools, since houses and ships were essential to their survival. And wood was abundant in the dense New England forests. They did not need to conserve materials, nor did they have the tools, the time, or the skills to work the materials into delicate spindles and thin boards. So the "Pilgrim" furniture from this time was heavily built, a rustic reflection of Jacobean design.

As the population of the colonies grew, furniture-making split into two factions: town and country. By the mid-1600s, there were nearly 40 towns in America and 24,000 people living in them. Some of the craftsmen in these towns (especially Boston, New York, Newport, and Philadelphia) began to specialize in cabinetmaking, building furniture for the well-to-do. They imported tools and copied the latest styles from Europe — William & Mary, Queen Anne, Chippendale. The pieces that were produced by these craftsmen later became known as "classic" American furniture.

But out in the rural areas and close to the frontier, furnituremaking continued in a tradition similar to that of the medieval joiners. During the warm seasons, farmers and pioneers cleared the land, planted crops, and built cabins and barns. When the weather drove them indoors, they made furniture and other implements for their own use, working with the same tools and materials they used to build their homes. The old English/Jacobean forms were simplified and mixed with designs brought by immigrants from other European countries. This blend of styles is what we now call "country" furniture.

Defining the Country Style

Country furniture is "folk" furniture. The craftsmen who built it made little or no attempt to follow the prevailing tastes and styles of the day. And because so many different folk traditions intermingled in America, there was no common design or system of construction that set country furniture apart from other furniture. You can tell a Queen Anne table or a Chippendale highboy from the forms that the cabinetmaker used to build it —cabriole legs, ogee moldings, bonnet tops, and so forth. But there are no distinct forms that identify country furniture. In fact, some country pieces may incorporate one or more of the classic forms just mentioned.

What defines country furniture is not a design, but what can best be called a *personality*. You can spot a piece of country furniture because of its practicality, ingenuity, or individuality.

Practicality — The farmers and pioneers who made country furniture were a practical people, out of necessity. They were not adverse to decorating a piece of furniture; many country pieces incorporate ornate fretwork, molding, and painted designs. Although country furniture may be highly decorated, its purpose is rarely *decorative*. Function was all-important, and this dictated the form of the piece.

Consider the dry sink in this book. The piece is completely practical; every part had an important function. The cabinet provided a place for storing extra buckets of water and kept dirt and soot from falling in the buckets. The splashboards around the top kept the water from spilling onto the floor. Even the curves of the splashboards had a function, although they added some decoration to the piece. The front splashboard had a low profile to make it easier to lift buckets into the sink. The back was higher because water was more likely to splash in this direction when you set a bucket down.

Ingenuity — Early cabins and farmhouses were small because they took less time to build and were easier to heat. Space was at a premium, and the inhabitants developed many ingenious pieces of furniture to save space. Trestle tables could be knocked down and stored against a wall. Window shelves made use of space that was otherwise unusable. Some pieces, like the dough box, performed two or more functions.

Life was hard on the frontier, and the farmers and pioneers also applied their ingenuity to save themselves work. Take a look at another example from this book: the pouting chair. Despite the fancy name, this piece is really a kitchen stool. The cut-out back is a *handle,* so that you can move the stool from place to place without having to stoop over.

Individuality — Even though their life was harder and their tools cruder than their urban counterparts, the rural craftsmen who made country furniture had a unique advantage. They did not have to cater to anybody's tastes but their own.

For the most part, they made furniture to be used only by themselves or members of their families. They rarely had to worry about whether or not their handiwork would sell. They were free to use any method of construction they felt comfortable with, or to incorporate any forms or styles that caught their fancy. More often than not, they customized pieces to fill a particular space or perform a particular function within their own homes.

For these reasons, you can't define the country style the same way you can other furniture styles. You can't find a "typical" country dry sink or hutch; even though you might be able to find elements of ethnic folk and classical woodworking designs in individual pieces. But there is nothing to tie them together as a genre; nothing, perhaps, except that elusive country "personality."

Country Materials

The forests of the New World (east of the Mississippi) offered twenty-six common species of wood suitable for furnituremaking, and the country craftsman used them all. While almost any wood could be used to build any piece of furniture, some woods were commonly used for specific purposes. Cherry, walnut, and figured maple were "formal" woods. Pieces of furniture built from these materials were often meant to be the focal point of a room. Durable woods such as hickory, oak, birch, and rock maple were used for utilitarian furniture that was expected to see a lot of heavy use. Informal and lightly used furniture was often built from poplar or ash.

The favorite wood of the country craftsman was white pine. It was abundant, easy to work, and surprisingly durable for its light weight and low density. So many pieces of country furniture were made from this wood that eighteenth and early nineteenth century American furniture designs used to be called "knotty pine" furniture. Some lumberyards even list it as "early American pine" in their inventories.

If wood was abundant, hardware was scarce. For most of the seventeenth century, the only metal in America was what the settlers imported from Europe. The earliest furniture built in this country was held together with wooden pegs and wedges. Hinges were often just strips of leather.

Even after the settlers built their own foundries and smithies, certain types of metal hardware remained scarce in the rural areas. Screws, for example, were more expensive to make than nails, and there was little use for them on a farm. Consequently, much country furniture was nailed together.

The choice of finishes available to the country cabinet-maker was as limited as the hardware. The earliest pieces went unfinished. Later on, craftsmen rubbed their furniture with linseed oil or a mixture of beeswax and turpentine.

As colored pigments became available, many pieces of furniture were painted. There was a lot of wood in a settler's life, and a brightly-colored painted chair or chest gave him some relief from the monotony of wood tones. (This is hard to understand in these modern times, where warm wood tones offer some relief from the monotony of colored plastics.) Painted furniture became a flourishing form of American folk art. Many pieces were decorated with stencils, toll-paintings, and marbleizing. Some pieces were even "wood grained"; that is, painted to look like exotic, imported woods or intricate marquetry and parquetry.

The Decline of Country Furniture — and New Beginnings

Most furniture scholars mark the last half of the nineteenth century as the end of country furniture — folk furniture produced in rural American farms and villages. The Industrial Revolution and mass-produced, mass-marketed furniture made it possible for all but the poorest farmers and villagers to buy their furniture "ready made." Country craftsmen, who built one-at-a-time, "made to order" furniture in the ancient tradition of the joiners, couldn't compete with the new furniture factories. One by one, these craftsmen closed up shop.

But the industrial methods that made it possible to mass produce furniture also made it possible to mass produce tools. Specialized woodworking tools — drills, jointers, routers, all sorts of saws and sanders — soon became commonplace. By the middle of the twentieth century, there were hundreds of thousands of "home workshops" in the garages and basements of America. In these shops, made-to-order woodworking and one-at-a-time craftsmanship continues as it has for centuries.

The reasons are different. Making your own furniture is no longer a necessity. Some of us do it to save money; others for the satisfaction of making something with our own hands; still others to make something better than we can buy. But the results are the same. We borrow a design here, a technique there, mix in some of our own ideas, and presto! Another one-of-a-kind piece of American furniture, tailor-made for the people who will use it.

Think of this as you build the projects in this book. *We* are the new country craftsmen and craftswomen.

These four pieces of furniture — a trestle table, two "Carver's" chairs, and a "court cupboard" — were all built around 1650. They are among the earliest pieces of furniture produced in this country. The court cupboard, with its heavy mortise-and-tenon construction, is a classic example of the Jacobean style.

Courtesy of the Metropolitan Museum of Art. All four pieces are gifts of Mrs. Russell Sage, 1909-1910.

Knife Caddy

Country folk had all sorts of carry-alls and containers to help them organize their lives — baskets, bowls, boxes, buckets, pouches, purses, scuttles — the list is almost endless. The "knife caddy" was one of the more formal and substantial receptacles on this list.

The knife caddy looks like a small toolbox or "tote." Originally, it was intended for carrying eating utensils from the kitchen to the dining room and back again. However, it proved to have thousands of other uses. Most country homes had several of these knife caddies filled with everything from sewing notions to gardening tools.

Today, the knife caddy remains just as versatile as it ever was. The dimensions shown here are just suggestions; you can custom-build this project to carry or hold all sorts of household items. Here are a few possible uses: condiment tray, fruit bowl, knitting holder, planter, and breadbasket. Use it, too, as an organizer or catch-all for thousands of small things such as buttons, coins, receipts, keys, coupons, and so on. You might even make one to use as a knife caddy.

Materials List

FINISHED DIMENSIONS

PARTS

A. Sides (2) ½" x 4¹/₃₂" x 15¾"
B. Ends (2) ½" x 4¹/₃₂" x 12"
C. Divider ½" x 8" x 15¾"
D. Bottom ¼" x 10½" x 14¼"
E. Dowels (30) ³/₁₆" dia. x 1"

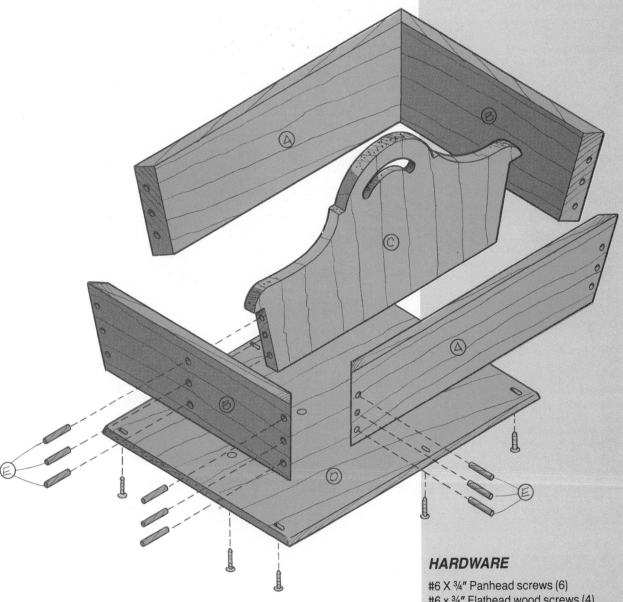

EXPLODED VIEW

HARDWARE

#6 X ¾" Panhead screws (6)
#6 x ¾" Flathead wood screws (4)
Felt (three ½" x 10" strips, or ten ¾"-dia. circles)

1 **_Cut the parts to size._**   Surface the wood you'll need to make the knife caddy to the thicknesses needed — ¼″ and ½″. Plane some scrap wood to ½″ thick so that you have about twice as much ½″ stock as you need. You'll need this extra scrap stock to test the compound miter setups. **Tip:** If you don't have a planer, many lumberyards and millwork operations will plane the stock you need for a small fee. You can also purchase

¼″- and ½″-thick stock from some mail-order wood-working supply houses.

Cut all the flat parts — sides, ends, divider, and bottom — slightly oversize, about ½″ longer and wider than the finished dimensions shown in the Materials List. You'll want this extra stock when it comes time to shape and fit the parts. From the ½″-thick scrap, cut two extra sides and two extra ends. These, too, should be oversize.

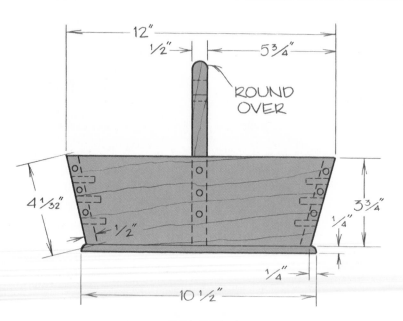

SIDE VIEW

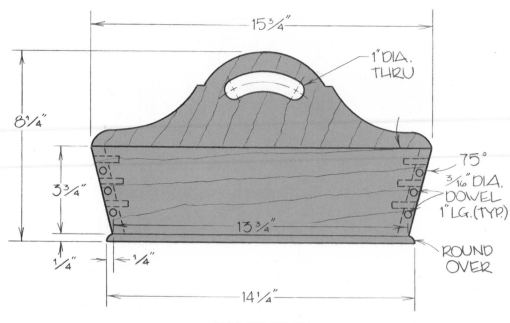

FRONT VIEW

2 Bevel and miter the sides and ends.

With your table saw blade tilted at 15°, bevel the top and bottom edges of the sides and ends (*both* the good parts and the scrap parts). These edges must be cut *parallel* to each other, as shown in the *Front View* and *Side View*.

The sides and ends are joined at the corners by "compound miters"; that is, the boards are simultaneously mitered *and* beveled. Make these compound miter cuts with the saw blade tilted at 43¼°, and the miter gauge angled at 75½°. (See Figure 1.) These angles are shown in the *Compound Miter & Bevel Cutting Details.*

Don't cut the good stock until you've first tested the blade and miter gauge setting on the scrap stock! These angle settings are straight out of a textbook, and only apply if your saw and saw blade are *perfectly* aligned and adjusted. When we made these cuts to build the knife caddy shown here, we had just aligned our table saw. Yet we still had to readjust the angles slightly to compensate for the idiosyncrasies of our machine.

Check the alignment of your saw and blade, then set the angles as shown. Compound-miter cut the sides and ends from the scrap wood. Dry assemble these scrap parts with masking tape. Check the corner joints and the angle of the sides. If the joints gap on the *outside, increase* the

1/Cut the compound miters in the sides and ends with the blade tilted at 43¼°, and the miter gauge angled at 75½°. These settings may vary slightly, depending on how your table saw is aligned and adjusted, so it's best to make some test cuts before you cut good wood.

blade tilt. If they gap on the *inside, reduce* the blade tilt. If the angle of the sides is *less* than 15° (off vertical), *reduce* the miter gauge angle (to less than 75½°). If the angle of the sides is *more* than 15°, *increase* the miter gauge angle. Make minute adjustments, not more than ¼° at a time.

Compound-miter cut the scrap ends and sides again to test the readjusted angles. Shave ¼" off the end of each board. Dry assemble the parts and check the fit. If necessary, adjust the blade tilt or the miter gauge angle again, and cut the scrap parts again. Keep doing this until you get a perfect fit. *Then* cut the good sides and ends.

**EDGE VIEW
SETTING FOR BLADE ANGLE**

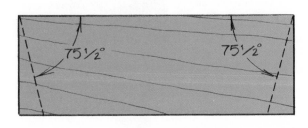

**FACE VIEW
SETTING FOR MITER GAUGE ANGLE**

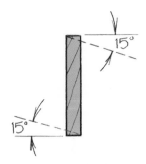

**END VIEW
SETTING FOR BLADE ANGLE**

COMPOUND MITER & BEVEL CUTTING DETAILS

3 Cut the shape of the divider.

Dry assemble the sides and ends, holding them together at the corner with masking tape or packing tape. Carefully measure the distance from end to end, along a top edge. The *Side View* shows the measurement to be 15¾", but this may have changed *slightly,* depending on how you cut the compound miters.

Enlarge the *Divider Pattern* and trace it onto the stock. Adjust the dimensions, if necessary, to fit the assembled sides and ends. Cut the outside shape with a band saw, jigsaw, or sabre saw.

> **TRY THIS!** Cut the shape of the divider ¹⁄₁₆" longer than needed, then carefully shave the stock with sandpaper or a fine rasp until the part fits perfectly. This takes longer, but you get a much better fit.

Make a "piercing cut" to create the opening for the handle. Drill two 1"-diameter holes at each end of the opening, then remove the waste between the holes with a sabre saw or jigsaw. Insert the blade of the saw in one of the holes and saw along the lines that you've marked. (See Figures 2 and 3.)

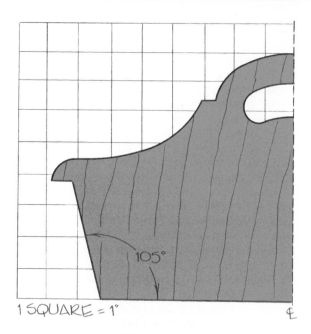

1 SQUARE = 1"

DIVIDER PATTERN

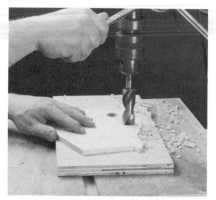

2/To pierce the handle, first drill two 1"-diameter holes through the divider stock. Back up each hole with a piece of hard scrap wood to prevent tear-out when the drill exits the stock.

3/Then remove the waste between the holes with a sabre saw. Insert the saw blade in one of the holes, and cut along the pattern lines.

> **TRY THIS!** If you have a 1"-diameter Forstener bit, or similar drill bit that cuts smooth-sided holes, drill four overlapping holes to make the opening for the handle. This was common practice among many country craftsmen. The sawtooth-effect that results where the holes overlap forms natural indentations for your fingers. It also adds a rustic, decorative look to the handle.

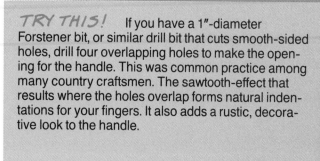

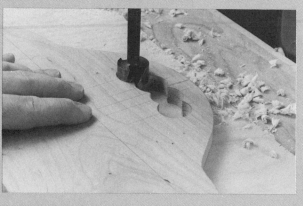

4

Cut the bottom. With the sides and ends still dry assembled and joined by tape, carefully measure the length and width across the bottom edges. The *Front View* and the *Side View* show these measurements at 13¾″ and 10″ respectively, but, once again, these may have changed slightly. After measuring, calculate how big the bottom should be by adding ½″ to both the length and width — this will allow for a ¼″ overhang on all sides. Cut the bottom to the sizes you've figured, and round over the edges.

5

Finish sand the parts. Remove the tape from the side/end assembly. Scrape and sand all the parts — sides, ends, divider, and bottom — to get them ready for assembly. Be careful to remove all the saw marks from the edges of the divider, on the top edge and where you've cut the shape of the handle.

6

Join the sides and ends. Apply glue to the adjoining surfaces of the ends and sides. Put the parts back together, taping the corners with fresh tape. While the tape holds the parts together, wrap two band clamps around the assembly, side-to-side and end-to-end, like a ribbon on a present. (See Figure 4.) Carefully tighten one band clamp just a little, then the second. Tighten the first a little more, then tighten the second again. Continue in this manner until you get the clamps as tight as you want them. They should be tight enough to keep the corner joints under pressure while the glue cures, but not so tight that the sides bow in. Let the glue cure, then remove the band clamps and the tape.

4/To hold the sides and ends together while the glue dries, wrap two band clamps around the assembly. These clamps should cross each other, like the ribbons on a gift-wrapped package. (If you don't have band clamps, you can also use strips of an old inner tube.)

7

Join the divider to the assembly. Spread glue on the ends of the divider, where it will join the assembly. Clamp it in place, with a band clamp wrapped around the assembly, end to end, and over the top of the divider. (See Figure 5.) Let the glue cure, then remove the band clamp.

5/Use a single band clamp to hold the divider to the caddy assembly while the glue dries. Wrap this clamp around the assembly and over the top edge of the divider.

8 Reinforce all the glue joints with dowels.

Drill ³/₁₆″-diameter, 1″-deep stopped dowel holes where the sides join the ends and where the ends join the divider, as shown in the *Front View* and *Side View*. Cut ³/₁₆″-diameter, 1¹/₁₆″-long dowels, coat them with glue, and drive them into the holes to reinforce the joints. (Later on, you'll sand these dowels to their proper length.)

Note that the dowels reinforcing the corners are driven from *both* directions, from the sides *and* from the ends, as shown in the *Corner Joinery Detail*. When you drill the holes for these corner dowels, the holes should *cross* at right angles (as you look at the assembly from the top), but they should *not intersect*.

TRY THIS! To make stopped holes precisely the right depth, use metal stop collars. Fasten these collars around the drill where you want to stop drilling. If you don't want to invest in collars, you can use a piece of masking tape instead to gauge the depth of a hole.

TRY THIS! For a "primitive" look, use nails (1″ brads) instead of dowels to reinforce the glue joints.

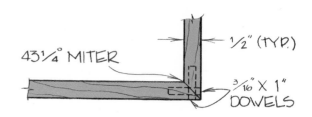

43¼° MITER   ½″ (TYP.)   ³/₁₆″ X 1″ DOWELS

CORNER JOINERY DETAIL

Step-by-Step: Routing Dovetail Key Joints

The corners of many knife caddies were joined with through dovetails. Because of the compound angles involved, these are quite difficult to do. However, if you have a router and a router table, you can make a decorative corner joint that looks very similar — a dovetail key joint.

1 **Secure the knife caddy assembly** in a V-jig so that one corner points down. Pass the jig across a dovetail bit, cutting a slot diagonally through the corner.

2 **Repeat, making several evenly-spaced slots** in each corner. These slots must not be so deep that they cut through to the inside of the caddy.

3 **Insert dovetail-shaped "keys"** in the slots, and glue them in place. Cut the keys off flush with the surface of the wood.

9 Attach the bottom to the assembly.

Attaching the bottom presents a problem: If you glue the bottom in place, or screw it tight to the assembly, the bottom will not be able to expand and contract with changes in humidity. The grain direction of the ends is perpendicular to the grain of the bottom, and this will restrict the movement of the bottom. Eventually, the bottom will split.

To prevent this, attach the bottom to the caddy with screws in *slots* instead of holes. You can still secure the bottom to the divider with flathead screws in ordinary countersunk pilot holes. However, use panhead screws in oversize counterbores and slots to attach the bottom to the sides, as shown in the *Bottom Layout* and *Counterbore and Slot Detail*. The bottom will be able to expand and contract from the middle.

To make the slotted counterbores, first drill ⅜"-diameter, ⅛"-deep holes. Inside these stopped holes, drill two or three ⅛"-diameter holes in a straight line, perpendicular to the grain direction, so that they form slots ⅛" wide and ¼" long. Drive #6 x ¾" panhead screws up through the slots in the bottom and into the sides, as shown in the *Bottom Joinery Detail*. Tighten the screws so that they are snug, but not so tight that they will restrict the movement of the bottom.

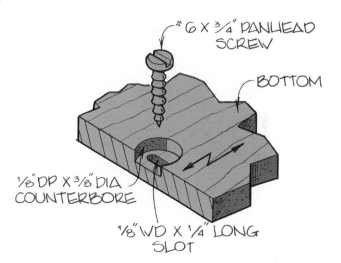

COUNTERBORE AND SLOT DETAIL

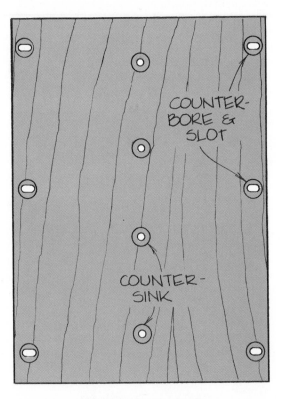

BOTTOM LAYOUT

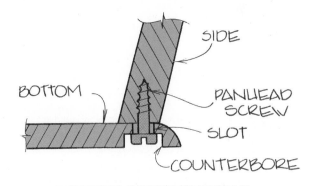

BOTTOM JOINERY DETAIL

10 Finish the caddy.

Sand the ends of the pegs flush with the surface of the sides and ends, and do any touch-up finish sanding that is still needed. Apply a finish to the completed caddy. Be sure to coat all sides evenly, and apply as many coats to the inside as you do the outside to prevent the assembly from warping or cupping. When the finish dries, glue strips or circles of felt to the underside of the caddy. This will hide the screws and protect the furniture that you will set this project on.

Porringer Serving Table

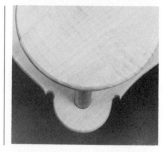

Although the porringer table is one of the most elegant country furniture forms, the term "porringer" has very humble beginnings.

It is a corruption and a combination of two words: the French "potage" (meaning soup), and the English "porridge." It was used to describe a small soup bowl with an oversize handle. Tradition has it that the *potage* bowl was a French invention, and the English adopted it to feed their children their daily *porridge.* The porringer was a common item in every English — and colonial English — nursery.

In the eighteenth century, country cabinetmakers began to build small tables with rounded, protruding corners. The reason for these corners is lost to us. Some scholars speculate that the protrusions were used to hold serving plates, but the more probable explanation is that some cabinetmakers rounded the corners of their tables so customers wouldn't bang their hips against them. As the style became popular, cabinetmakers exaggerated the round corner and made it a design element. These protruding corners reminded the country folk of the handle on a porringer, and the name stuck. Soon, "porringer tables" were a common sight in country kitchens and dining areas.

This particular table is a "serving porringer." There are two porringer-shaped surfaces — the table top and a smaller shelf below. Two-tiered tables were often used beside dining tables to hold the food at ready, and keep the main table uncluttered. They were useful in the kitchen, too. The table top offered extra workspace, and the shelf held much-used utensils where they would be out of the way, yet right at hand. ✳

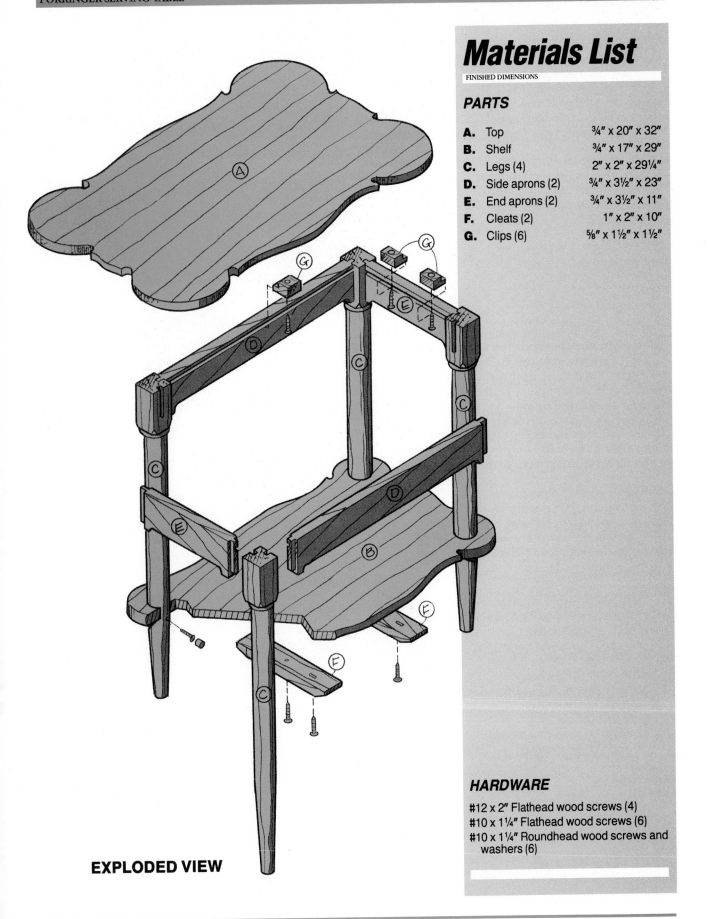

Materials List

FINISHED DIMENSIONS

PARTS

A.	Top	¾" x 20" x 32"
B.	Shelf	¾" x 17" x 29"
C.	Legs (4)	2" x 2" x 29¼"
D.	Side aprons (2)	¾" x 3½" x 23"
E.	End aprons (2)	¾" x 3½" x 11"
F.	Cleats (2)	1" x 2" x 10"
G.	Clips (6)	⅝" x 1½" x 1½"

HARDWARE

#12 x 2" Flathead wood screws (4)
#10 x 1¼" Flathead wood screws (6)
#10 x 1¼" Roundhead wood screws and
   washers (6)

EXPLODED VIEW

1

Cut all parts to size. To make this table, you'll need approximately 12 board feet of 4/4 ("four-quarters") stock, surfaced to ¾" thick; 4 turning squares, 2" x 2" x 32", and some 10"-long scraps of 1"-thick hardwood. If you don't have the hardwood scraps, you can glue up the stock from the 4/4 waste, and resaw it to size.

Glue up the wide stock you need to make the top and the shelf; then cut the ¾"-thick and 1"-thick parts — top, shelf, aprons, and cleats — to the sizes shown in the Materials List. Do not cut the legs or the clips just yet.

TRY THIS! Consider making your porringer table out of two contrasting woods — one for the top and the shelf, and another for the legs, aprons, and other parts. Country cabinetmakers often mixed woods for effect. The table in this chapter is made from curly "tiger" maple and wild cherry. Other good-looking combinations include cherry and walnut, butternut and walnut, birch and cherry, ash and red oak, white oak and hickory, sassafras and poplar. Use one of these or another combination of domestic woods that are particularly eye-catching.

2

Cut the joinery in the legs and aprons. The aprons are joined to the legs by slot mortises and tenons. Cut these joints *before* you shape or turn these parts. It's much easier to make a well-fitted joint while the stock is still square.

Cut the slot mortises in the legs first. Mount a ⅜"-straight bit in your router, and mount the router in a router table. Clamp a fence on the table to guide the stock, and clamp a stop block to the fence to stop the cut. Keeping the leg pressed tightly against the fence, cut a mortise ⅜" wide, ½" deep, and 3" long. (See Figure 1.) The mortise should be cut in an *inside* face of the stock, ¹¹/₁₆" from the adjacent *outside* face, as shown in the *Leg-to-Apron Joinery Detail.* Turn the leg 90°, and cut a second slot in the other inside face. Repeat for all the legs.

1/Rout the mortises in the legs before you turn the legs. Use a straight bit, and mount your router in a router table. Feed the legs into the bit so that the rotation of the bit helps hold them against the fence.

TRY THIS! Do not rout the entire ½"-deep slot in one pass — the stock will burn and the bit will dull quickly. Instead, rout the slot in several passes, cutting ⅛"–¼" deeper with each pass. In addition, feed the stock into the cutter so that the rotation of the cutter keeps the stock pressed against the fence. This will help keep the slot mortise perfectly straight.

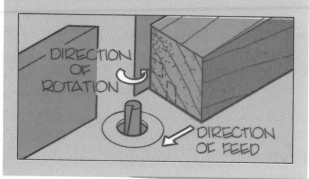

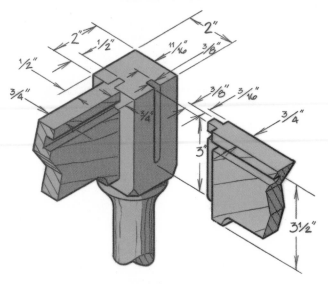

LEG-TO-APRON JOINERY DETAIL

You can cut the tenons in the ends of the aprons with the same setup. Remove the stop block and readjust the position of the fence so that when you pass the ¾″-thick stock between the fence and the bit, you'll cut a rabbet ½″ wide and ³⁄₁₆″ deep. To make the tenons, cut one face, turn the board over, and cut the other. (See Figure 2.) With a band saw, or a coping saw, notch the lower edge of the tenons so that they're 3″ wide. Round the lower edge with a rasp to fit the mortises, as shown in the *Side Apron Layout* and *End Apron Layout*.

Finally, cut the grooves on the inside faces of the aprons. Readjust the position of the fence and make ⅜″-wide, ⅜″-deep grooves near the top edge of all the aprons.

Alternative method: If you don't have a router table, drill the mortises. Make a series of overlapping holes in the legs, then clean up the edges of the mortises with a chisel. Make the tenons with a hand-held router. Clamp the aprons together, edge to edge, and clamp a straight-

2/You can use the same routing setup to cut the tenons as you used to make the mortises.

edge to the aprons. Rout one side of the tenons, using the straightedge as a guide. Turn the aprons over and repeat. When you've made the tenons, use the router and an edge-guide to cut the grooves.

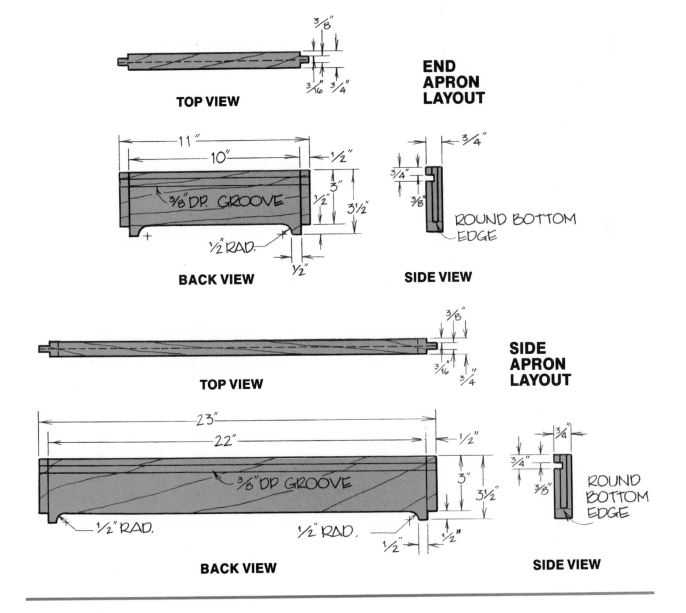

3 ***Turn the shape of the legs.*** Mount the legs on your lathe and turn the shape shown in the *Front View* and *Side View*. This shape is very simple, nothing more than a cylinder with a block at one end and a taper at the other. However, it does require some care. The cylinder must be turned *precisely* to 1⅜″ in diameter, and the taper must start no higher than 8¾″ from the lower end of the leg. If the diameter of the cylinder varies, or the taper starts higher than specified,

the shelf will not fit the legs properly. For more information on how to turn a cylinder to a precise diameter, refer to *Step-by-Step: Turning a Specific Diameter.*

Turn the legs so that all the waste is on the *bottom* end, opposite the end where you have cut the mortises. Sand the turned legs smooth on the lathe, then cut off the waste. Be sure you make all four legs precisely the same length.

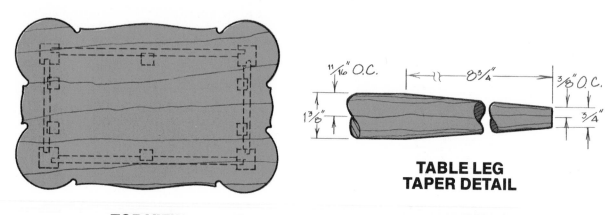

TOP VIEW

TABLE LEG TAPER DETAIL

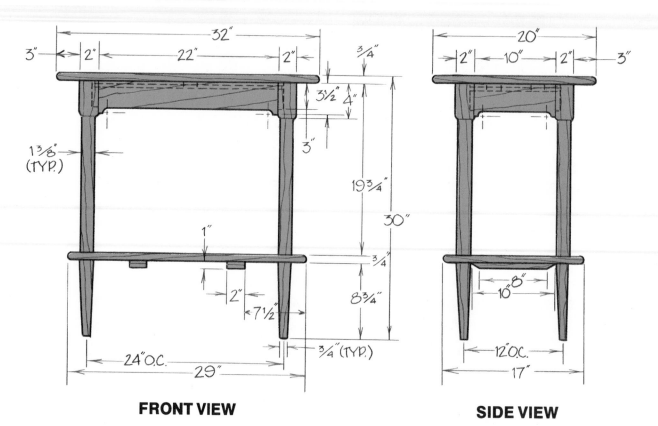

FRONT VIEW   **SIDE VIEW**

4 **Cut the shape of the aprons.** With a band saw or a sabre saw, cut the shape of the lower edge in each of the aprons. Sand away the saw marks. A small drum sander and a strip sander make short work of this chore.

Step-by-Step: Turning a Specific Diameter

Turning a round tenon or a leg to a specific diameter requires a good deal of patience and precision. However, you can make this chore a lot simpler by using a simple "turning gauge" that you make yourself from scrap wood. This turning gauge is actually a fixed caliper for that specific diameter. Shown here is the layout for the gauge you need to turn the legs for the *Porringer Serving Table.*

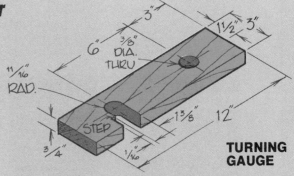

TURNING GAUGE

1 **Round the stock** to a rough diameter using ordinary calipers. Set your calipers at least ⅛″ larger than the final diameter you want to turn. Round the waste at the end of the legs, too, but turn this waste to a diameter ⅛″ smaller than the final diameter of the legs. Do this so that you can later fit the gauge over the legs to check the fit of the stock in the hole.

2 **Continue turning,** removing minute amounts of stock. Check your work frequently with the turning gauge. When the gauge slips over the work up to the "step," stop turning immediately. If the gauge slips over the turning and past the step, you've removed too much stock.

3 **Set your chisels aside** and begin to sand the stock. Continue checking the diameter of the turning with the gauge. When the gauge slips past the step, stop sanding.

4 **Check the fit** of the tenon or the leg by removing the turning from the lathe and inserting it in the hole in the gauge. If the fit is too tight, put the turning back on the lathe and continue sanding with very fine sandpaper. Remove the stock and check the fit again. When you finally get the fit you want, don't sand the stock any more except to smooth it with fine steel wool.

5 Cut the shape of the top and the shelf.

Enlarge the *Top Pattern* and *Shelf Pattern,* and trace them on the stock. Drill ⅞″-diameter holes through the top stock and ⅝″-diameter holes through the shelf stock, where shown in the patterns. With a holesaw, cut 1⅜″-diameter holes through the shelf near each of the corners. Then cut the long curves in the stock with a sabre saw. Sand away the saw marks. As you sand, be careful to maintain "fair" curves. Don't dwell in any place too long with the sander to avoid making dips and flat spots.

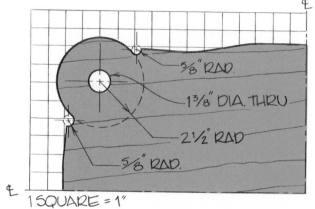

TOP PATTERN

7/8″ RAD.

4″ RAD.

7/8″ RAD.

1 SQUARE = 1″

SHELF PATTERN

5/8″ RAD.

1⅜″ DIA. THRU

2½″ RAD

5/8″ RAD.

1 SQUARE = 1″

6 Shape the edge of the top and the shelf.

With a router and a piloted ⅜″ quarter-round bit, round over both the bottom and the top edge of the top and the shelf. Adjust the depth of cut on your router to ¼″, so that there is a flat spot on the edge between the quarter-round shapes, as shown in the *Edge Detail.* (This flat provides solid support for the pilot when you round over both the top and bottom edges.) Sand away the flats, blending them with the rounded edges, creating oval-shaped edges.

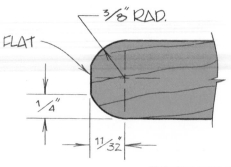

FLAT

3/8″ RAD.

1/4″

11/32″

EDGE DETAIL

7 Cut the joinery in the cleats.

The cleats brace the shelf and keep it from cupping. However, the shelf must also be allowed to expand and contract with changes in temperature and humidity. To facilitate this, the cleats are attached to the shelves with screws in *slotted* holes.

To make the cleats, first cut chamfers across the ends of the cleats, as shown in the *Side View* and *Cleat Layout.* In each cleat, drill three counterbored pilot holes for #10 roundhead wood screws. Make the middle pilot hole round, 3/16″ in diameter, and the end pilot holes slotted, 3/16″ wide x ½″ long. To create these slots, drill several 3/16″-diameter holes in the bottom of the counterbores, all in a line parallel with the grain direction. Then drill out the waste between the holes. (See Figure 3.)

3/To make the slotted pilot holes in the cleats, first drill the counterbore on your drill press. Then drill a series of 3/16″-diameter overlapping holes inside the counterbore. Remove the waste between these holes by advancing and retracting the drill bit on the press.

8

Make the clips. Sand or surface a piece of hardwood scrap to approximately ⅝″ thick. *Across* one end, cut a ⅜″-wide, ⁷⁄₁₆″-deep rabbet. Crosscut the rabbeted end to a length of 1½″, then rip that stock into 1½″ squares. (See Figure 4.) Repeat, if necessary, so that you have six clips for fastening the top to the aprons.

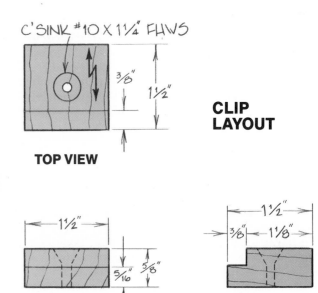

CLIP LAYOUT

TOP VIEW

FRONT VIEW

SIDE VIEW

4/To make the clips, cut a rabbet across the end of a board, then cut the clips from the board. Important: The grain direction of the clips must be perpendicular to the rabbet. Otherwise, the clips may break.

9

Finish sand all parts. To get ready to assemble the table, finish sand all the parts you have made. If you have followed normal turning procedures, you will have sanded the legs on the lathe. However, you may wish to lightly sand them *with* the grain. Be careful not to remove too much stock with the sandpaper, especially in the areas where the shelf and legs meet.

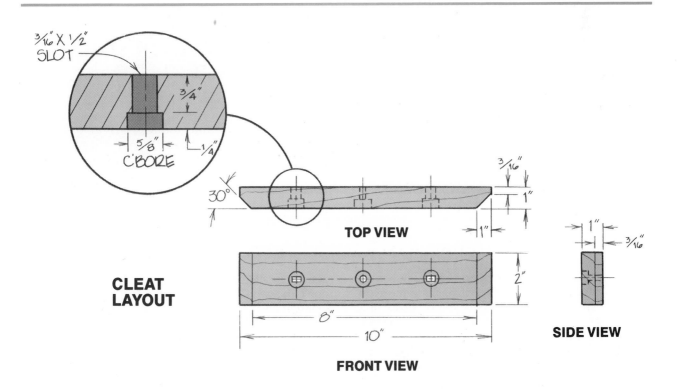

CLEAT LAYOUT

TOP VIEW

FRONT VIEW

SIDE VIEW

10

Assemble the table. Glue the legs to the aprons, inserting the tenons in the mortises. As you clamp up the leg/apron assembly, be absolutely sure that it is square. After the glue dries, turn the assembly upside down. Tighten a handscrew clamp to each leg, 19¾″ from the top edge of the assembly. Be careful not to mar the wood. Fit the shelf over the legs and let it rest on the handscrews. Fasten the shelf in place with #12 x 2″ flathead wood screws, one per leg. Drill the pilot holes for these screws at a slight angle, so that the screws will pass through the leg from the "inside" surface, under the shelf, and part way into the shelf, as shown in the *Shelf-to-Leg Joinery Detail.* Counterbore and countersink the screws, then cover the heads with plugs. Sand the plugs flush with the surface of the wood to make them as inconspicuous as possible. (See Figures 5 and 6.)

Fasten the cleats to the underside of the shelf with #10 x 1¼″ roundhead wood screws and washers. You can tighten the screws in the middle holes as much as you want, but just "snug up" the screws in the end (slotted) holes, so that the shelf stock is free to expand and contract with changes in the weather. *Do not* glue the cleats to the shelf.

Finally, fasten the top to the aprons with the clips. Attach each clip to the top with a #10 x 1¼″ flathead wood screw. Note that there will be a small gap under

each clip, as shown in the *Top-to-Apron Joinery Detail.* This gap is necessary. Without it, the clips might not hold the top tight against the aprons. As with the screws in the ends of the cleats, just snug up the clips; don't tighten them down too much. The top, too, must be free to swell and shrink. (See Figure 7.)

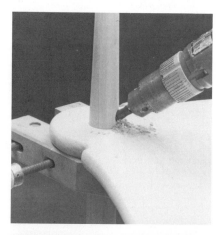

5/Drill the pilot holes for the screws that hold the shelf to the legs at a slight angle. Work from the inside surface of the leg, under the shelf. With your free hand, feel the outside surface of the leg and the top of the shelf. If you should sense a vibration, this means the bit is about to exit the wood. Stop drilling immediately. You don't want to see the screw hole above the shelf.

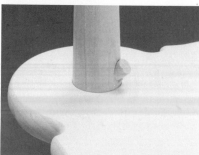

6/With a plug cutter, make plugs to cover the heads of the screws. So that the grain of the plugs matches the legs, save the waste from the end of the leg stock and cut the plugs from these.

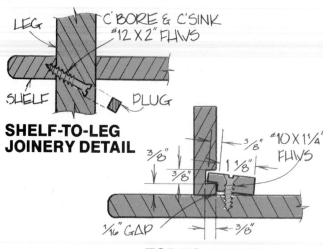

SHELF-TO-LEG JOINERY DETAIL

LEG
C'BORE & C'SINK #12 X 2″ FHWS
SHELF
PLUG

#10 X 1¼″ FHWS
3/8″
1 1/8″
3/8″
3/8″
3/8″
1/16″ GAP
3/8″

TOP-TO-APRON JOINERY DETAIL

7/Arrange the clips to hold the top flat on the aprons. If you live in a humid climate, you may want to use two clips at each corner. This will prevent cupping.

11

Finish the completed table. When you're satisfied that everything fits, remove the top, clips, and cleats from the leg/apron/shelf assembly. Be sure to mark the positions of the clips and cleats so that you can put everything back in the proper place.

Apply a finish to the parts of the table. Be careful to brush on or wipe on just as many coats to the underside

of the tops and shelves as you do to the top side. If you don't, the two sides will absorb and release moisture at different rates, and the parts will tend to warp or cup. This, in turn, may distort the table. After the finish is dry and you've rubbed it to the lustre you want, reassemble the table.

Pie Safe

The "pie safe" is the country cabinetmaker's solution to a cook's dilemma.

The country cook believed, as cooks had for centuries, that food was best stored in the fresh air. Food stored in stagnant or "bad" air would go stale or spoil. The cook knew, however, that food left out in the open was in danger of assault by any number of pests: insects, rodents, and small hungry boys, just to name a few.

So the country cabinetmaker built this ventilated cabinet, a direct descendant of medieval food cupboards. The panels on the doors and sides of a typical pie safe were made from punched tin or copper. (Because of the metal panels, these cabinets were also called "tin safes." After the invention of wire screen, some were known as "wire safes.") The holes in the metal were numerous enough to let the air circulate around the food inside the cabinet, but small enough to keep out all but the tiniest of critters. Often, the holes were punched in a pattern, adding decoration to the otherwise utilitarian cupboard.

The designs frequently had some significance. Either the punched holes formed a traditional folk motif, such as the "American Eagle" pattern you see on the pie safe shown here, or they incorporated shapes that had some religious meaning for the people who made them. We've provided several different designs and explanations of their significance for you to choose from when you build your pie safe. You can also copy other patterns that you've seen elsewhere — or design your own.

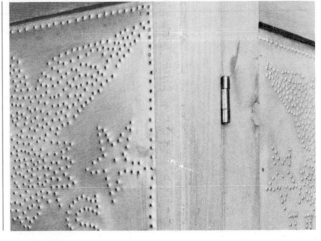

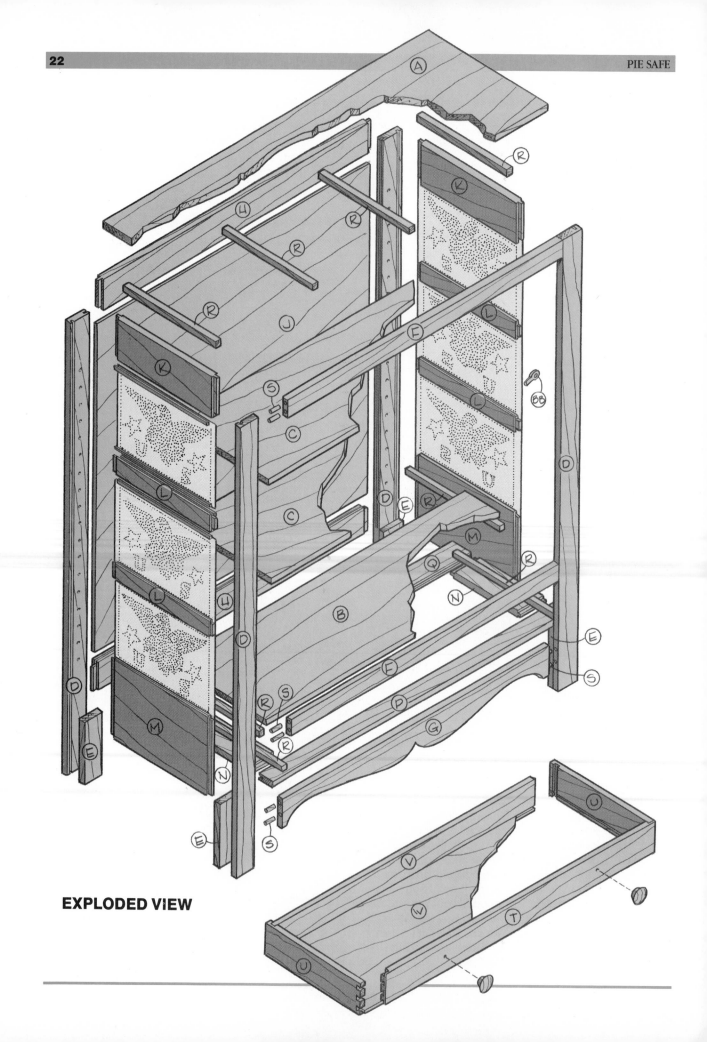

EXPLODED VIEW

DOORS
EXPLODED VIEW

Materials List

FINISHED DIMENSIONS

PARTS

A.	Top	3/4″ x 16½″ x 45¾″
B.	Bottom	3/4″ x 13½″ x 41¼″
C.	Adjustable shelves (2-3)	3/4″ x 13⅜″ x 41⅛″
D.	Stiles (4)	3/4″ x 2¾″ x 53½″
E.	Short legs (4)	3/4″ x 2¾″ x 8″
F.	Top/middle face rails (2)	3/4″ x 2″ x 37¼″
G.	Skirt	3/4″ x 3¾″ x 37¼″
H.	Back rails (2)	3/4″ x 3½″ x 38″
J.	Back	¼″ x 38″ x 39¼″
K.	Side top rails (2)	3/4″ x 4½″ x 14¼″
L.	Side middle rails (4)	3/4″ x 2″ x 14¼″
M.	Side bottom rails (2)	3/4″ x 9¼″ x 14¼″
N.	Web frame rails (2)	3/4″ x 3½″ x 10″
P.	Web frame front stile	3/4″ x 1¾″ x 41¼″
Q.	Web frame back stile	3/4″ x 2½″ x 41¼″
R.	Drawer guides/ cleats (8)	3/4″ x 3/4″ x 13½″
S.	Dowels (12)	⅜″ dia. x 2″
T.	Drawer front	3/4″ x 3⅞″ x 37⅛″
U.	Drawer sides (2)	3/4″ x 3⅞″ x 14″
V.	Drawer back	3/4″ x 3⅞″ x 36⅜″
W.	Drawer bottom	¼″ x 13⅛″ x 36⅜″
X.	Outside door stiles (2)	3/4″ x 2½″ x 36⅝″
Y.	Inside door stiles (2)	3/4″ x 2⅞″ x 36⅝″
Z.	Top/bottom door rails (4)	3/4″ x 2½″ x 18⅞″
AA.	Middle door rails (4)	3/4″ x 2″ x 14¼″
BB.	Latch	3/4″ x 1¼″ x 3¼″

HARDWARE

10″ x 14¼″ Sheet metal panels (12)*
Door/drawer pulls and mounting screws (4)
1½″ x 2″ Butt hinges and mounting screws
#10 x 1¼″ Roundhead wood screw and washer
#8 x 1¼″ Flathead wood screws (36-48)
Shelving supports (8-12)

*Available from heating and air conditioning contractors who make their own ducts. When you purchase these panels, you'll quickly find that there is no longer any such thing as "tin." The closest you'll be able to come is galvanized steel or aluminum. Some pie safes were made with sheet copper, and this is still available — but it's very expensive.

1

Cut the parts to size. Glue up the solid
wood stock you need to make the wide parts —
top, bottom, and shelves. Then rip, crosscut, and joint all
the parts to the sizes shown in the Materials List. Before
you cut, be sure that your saw and jointer are properly

aligned and adjusted so that you get precise, square cuts.
Square edges and ends are extremely important when
making large case projects such as this. Even a small
deviation from square will throw the case out of kilter.

2

Cut the shape of the bottom front rail.
Enlarge the *Skirt Pattern* and trace it on the stock.
Cut the shape of the skirt with a band saw, scroll saw, or
sabre saw. Sand away the saw marks from the sawn edge.

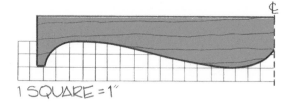

1 SQUARE = 1"

SKIRT PATTERN

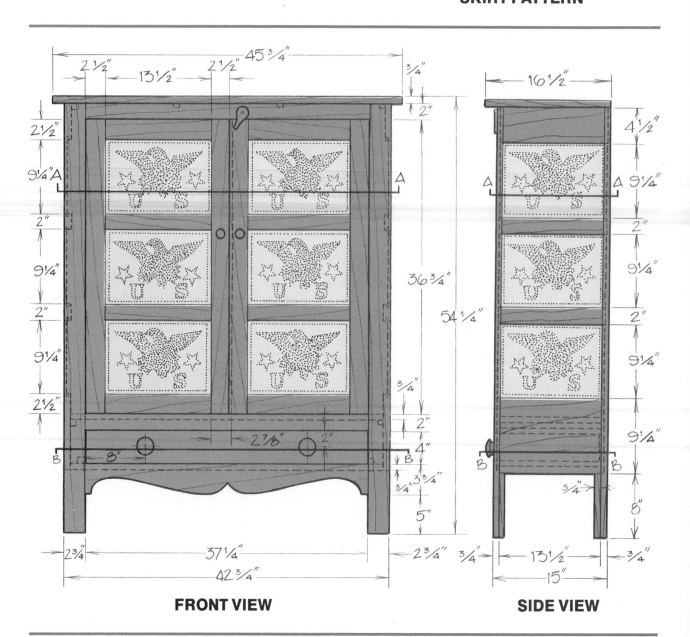

FRONT VIEW　　　　　　　　　　　**SIDE VIEW**

3 Drill the holes for shelving supports in the stiles.

Lay out the locations of the holes for adjustable shelving supports on the inside of the stile, as shown in the *Stile Layout.* Drill stopped holes in the stiles, ¼″ in diameter and ⅜″ deep.

4 Cut the grooves in the rails and stiles.

The pie safe case is joined with tenons and grooves, for the most part. There are a lot of them, but they can all be made with the same tool setup. Mount a dado cutter in your table saw, and set it up to cut a groove ¼″ wide and ⅜″ deep. Position the rip fence ¼″ away from the cutter. With this setup, cut the grooves in the stiles, web frame stiles, door stiles, side rails, back rails, and door rails.

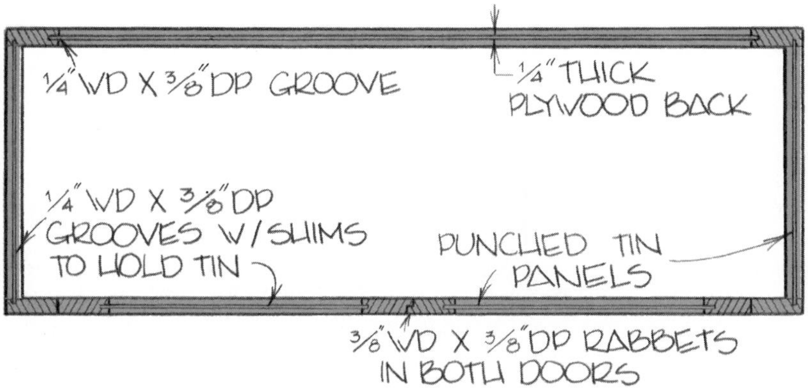
1/4" WD X 3/8" DP GROOVE
1/4" THICK PLYWOOD BACK
1/4" WD X 3/8" DP GROOVES W/SHIMS TO HOLD TIN
PUNCHED TIN PANELS
3/8" WD X 3/8" DP RABBETS IN BOTH DOORS

SECTION A

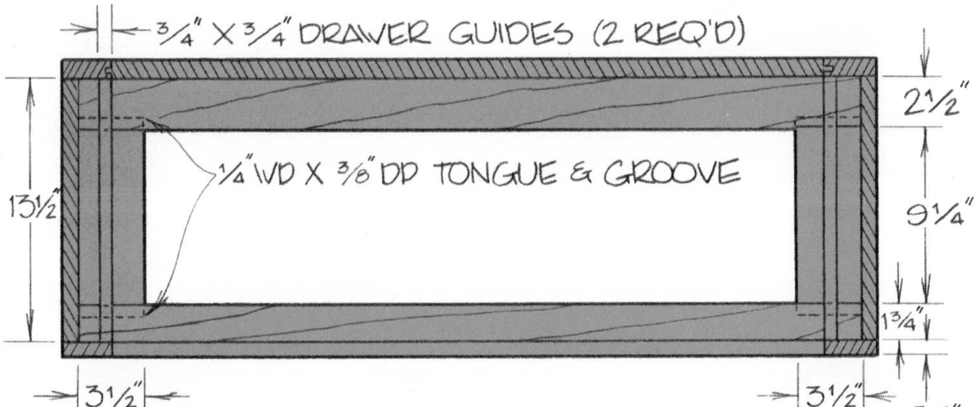
3/4" X 3/4" DRAWER GUIDES (2 REQ'D)
1/4" WD X 3/8" DP TONGUE & GROOVE
13 1/2"
2 1/2"
9 1/4"
1 3/4"
3/4"
3 1/2"
3 1/2"

SECTION B

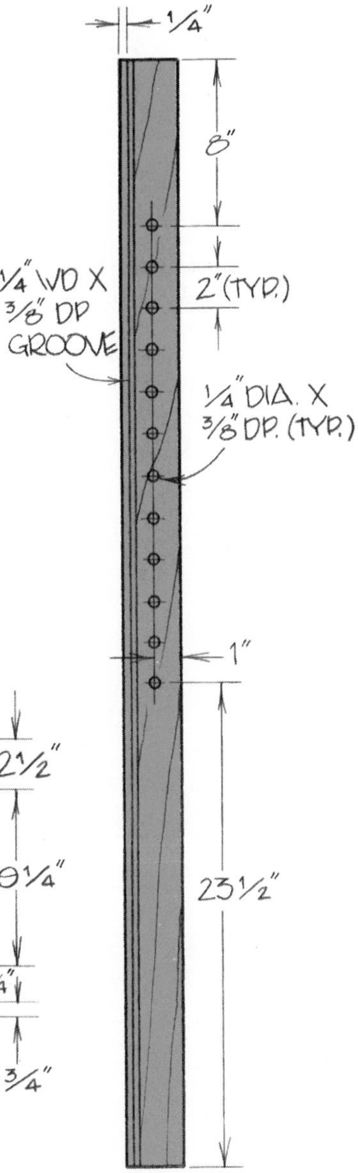
1/4"
8"
2"(TYP.)
1/4" WD X 3/8" DP GROOVE
1/4" DIA. X 3/8" DP. (TYP.)
1"
23 1/2"

STILE LAYOUT

5 Cut the tenons in the rails.

Remove or reposition the fence on your saw, but leave the dado cutter exactly as it is. With a tenoning jig, cut the tenons on the ends of the web frame rails, side rails, back rails, and middle door rails. (See Figure 1.) *Do not* cut the tenons in the top or bottom door rails at this time — these require a different setup.

Round the bottom corners of the tenons on the bottom side rails and bottom back rail. This roundover should be the same diameter as your dado cutter, so that the tenons will fit the blind grooves in the stiles. (See Figure 2.)

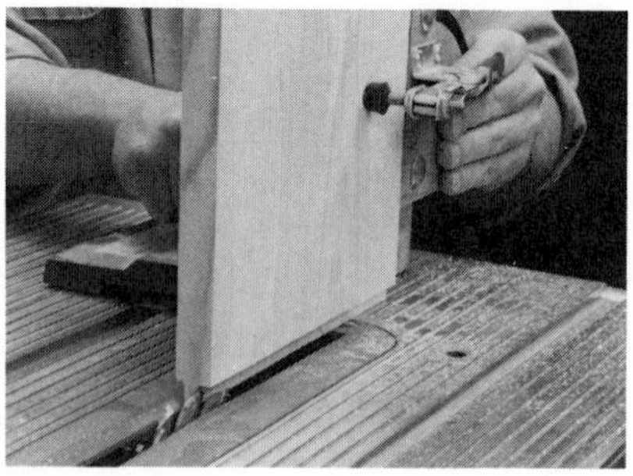

***1**/Use a tenoning jig to cut the tenons in the ends of the rails, and the slot mortises or "bridle" joints in the door stiles.*

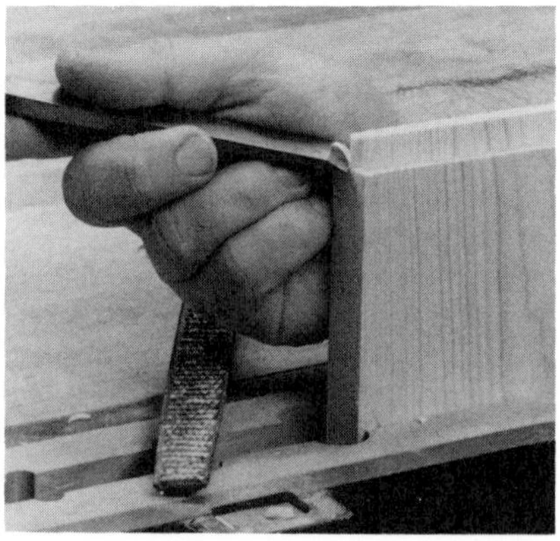

***2**/Round the bottom corners of the tenons on the bottom back rail and bottom side rail, so that the tenons will fit in the blind grooves.*

6 Cut the door frame joinery.

The door stiles and top/bottom rails are joined with open or "slot" mortises and tenons (also called "bridle" joints). While you still have the dado cutter mounted in your table saw, readjust the cutter to saw a 1/4"-wide groove, 2 1/8" deep. With the tenoning jig, cut the slot mortises in the ends of the door stiles.

> TRY THIS! If your dado cutter won't cut 2 1/8" deep, use a table saw blade and make several passes. You can also make the slot mortises with your band saw. Cut the sides of the mortise, then "nibble" away at the bottom with the blade until the corners of the slot are square.

Set up the dado cutter to cut 1/4" deep and as wide as it will go. Then cut the tenons on the top and bottom door rails, using the miter gauge to guide the cut. Since most dado cutters won't cut more than 13/16" wide, you'll have to make the tenons in several passes. Attach a stop block to your rip fence to stop the cut when the tenon is long enough. (See Figure 3.) Remember, the tenons should be made to two different lengths — 2 1/2" long on the *outside* end of the rails, and 2 7/8" long in the *inside* end of the rails.

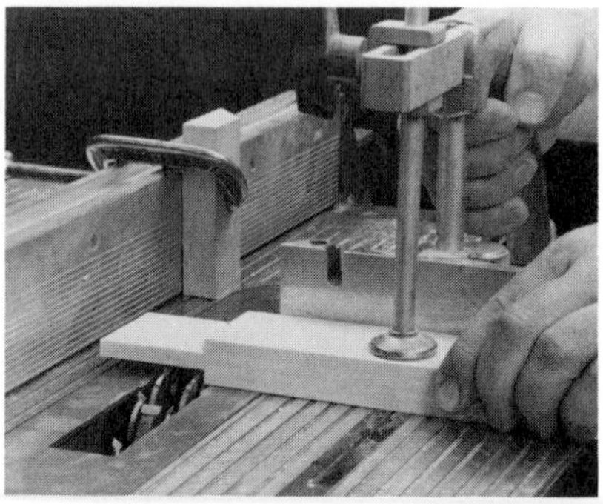

***3**/Attach a stop block to your rip fence to gauge the length of the tenons in the door rails.*

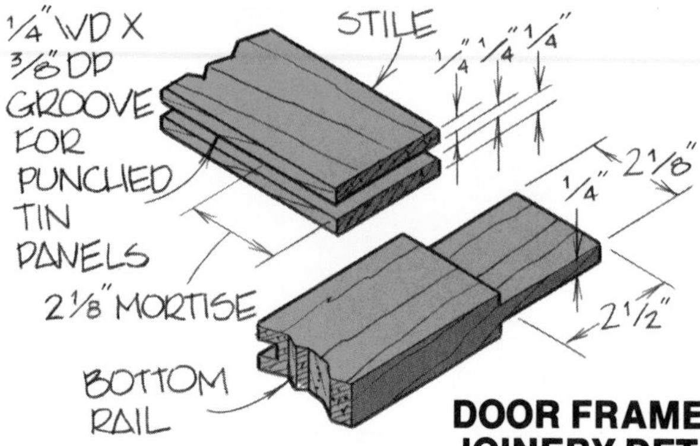
1/4" WD X 3/8" DP GROOVE FOR PUNCHED TIN PANELS
STILE
1/4" 1/4" 1/4"
2 1/8"
1/4"
2 1/8" MORTISE
2 1/2"
BOTTOM RAIL

DOOR FRAME JOINERY DETAIL

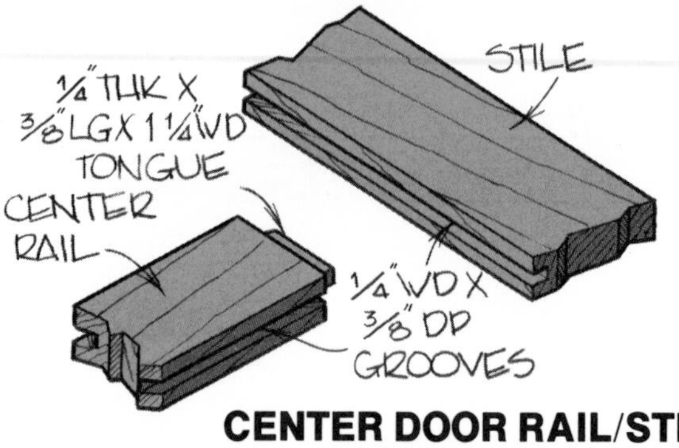
1/4" THK X 3/8" LG X 1 1/4" WD TONGUE
STILE
CENTER RAIL
1/4" WD X 3/8" DP GROOVES

CENTER DOOR RAIL/STILE JOINERY DETAIL

7
Join the parts for the front frame.
The face frame rails, stiles, and skirt are all joined with dowels. Drill the dowel holes with the aid of a doweling jig.

TRY THIS!   If you have a "biscuit machine," you can also use this to join the face frame parts.

8
Punch the sheet metal panels.   Select a pattern for the panels, or design your own. Enlarge the pattern to the proper size, and have a nearby "quick-print" business make a dozen photocopies. (Most post offices and libraries also have photocopy machines.) Mount the copied patterns to the sheet metal panels with a spray adhesive. (Spray adhesive, sometimes called Spray Mount, is available at most office supply, art supply, and photographic supply stores.)

Sharpen a long punch to make the holes and a cold chisel to make the slots. Place the first panel on a scrap of ¾"-thick plywood to provide a backing. Pull up a stool to your workbench, sit down, and get comfortable — it takes a long, long time to punch twelve metal panels. As you work, be careful not to drive the punch or the chisel too deep into the plywood backing. The tool will stick in the panel, and this will quickly tire you. Just hit the punch or the chisel hard enough to barely pierce the metal.

An historical note: Early pie safes were made with the tin punched *out*. This made it harder for the insects to find their way inside. However, it also made it harder to clean the metal panels. Later pie safe builders decided that cleanliness was more important than pest control, and punched the tin *in*.

TRY THIS!   To save some of the tedium of punching twelve identical panels, make a template from ¾" plywood. Drill ⅛" holes through the plywood wherever you want to punch holes in the metal. Then drive ⅞"-long roofing nails into but not through each of the holes. Place a metal panel on the plywood backing, then position the template over the panel. With a hammer, drive all of the roofing nails through the template and into the panel. They will only go ⅛" into the metal — just deep enough to pierce it. With a small pry bar, remove the template from the metal. Tap the points of the nails back up into the template, and repeat for another panel. The drawback to this method is that you can only make holes, not slots. And the holes must be fairly far apart — no closer than the radius of the heads of the roofing nails.

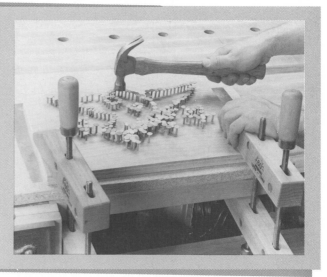

(1 SQUARE = 1")

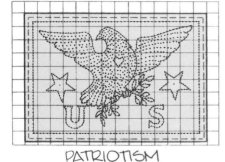

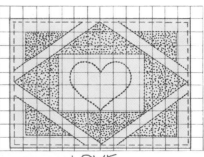

PATRIOTISM   HOSPITALITY   LOVE

OPTIONAL PATTERNS FOR PUNCHED METAL PANELS

9

Finish sand all parts. Scrape and sand all the wooden parts of the pie safe, to get them ready to finish. Be careful not to round over adjoining edges.

10

"Antique" the metal panels. If you bought galvanized steel or aluminum panels, chances are they are too shiny for your taste. They need to be artificially aged. There are several chemical solutions that will do this, but the easiest to use and most readily available is "gun bluing" — the same stuff you rub on the barrel of a rifle or a pistol to prevent it from rusting. This is available at most hunting supply stores. Just dab the bluing on the panels with cotton balls.

You may want to try "roasting" the panels. Build a nice, big campfire or fire in your fireplace, and set the panels in the midst of it. Be careful not to get the fire too hot; or the panels could melt. After a few minutes in the fire, the heat will discolor the metal, and make it look old.

There's one other option: Salvage some tin roofing from an old building that's being torn down, and make the panels from this.

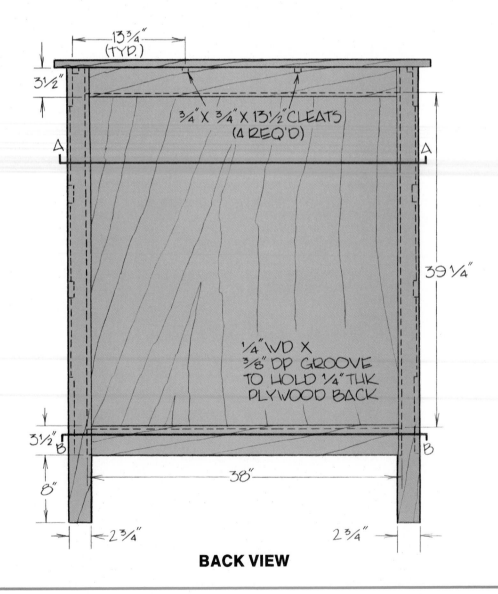

BACK VIEW

11

Assemble the frames. Assemble the face frame, back frame, web frame, and door frames, gluing the tenons in the grooves. *Do not* glue the metal or the plywood panels in place. Just let them float in the grooves. Attach the drawer guides to the web frame with glue and screws.

12

Assemble the case. Using glue and screws, join the face frame and the back frame with the top, bottom, web frame, side rails, and side panels. Get a helper to assist you in putting all these parts together — unless you have six arms and the patience of a saint.

First, glue the short feet in place on the inside surfaces of the back frame and face frame. While the glue cures, drill pilot holes in the cleats. You'll need two sets of holes in the end cleats — one set to attach the cleat to the top or bottom, and another set to attach the cleat to the inside of the case. Using the first set of holes, screw the cleats to the underside of the top and bottom. Countersink these screws so that the heads are flush with the surface of the stock.

Lay the back frame flat on the floor of your workshop, back surface down. Dry-assemble the side rails to the back frame, but do *not* slide the metal panels into their grooves yet. Put the web frame in place, then dry-assemble the face frame to the rails. Wrap band clamps around the case to hold the parts together. Drive screws through the web frame into the short legs. Put the bottom in place, and drive screws through the cleats in the side bottom rails (using the second set of pilot holes).

Disassemble the case, and reassemble it with screws *and* glue. Work fast; you must finish this assembly before the glue sets up. Slide the metal panels in place just before you fit the face frame to the assembly. Glue the web frame to the side bottom rails, but do *not* drive screws through the rails into the frame to hold them together. When you finish assembling the case, there should be no screws showing on the outside.

Hold the assembly together with band clamps and bar clamps, then stand the case up on its legs. Fit the top to the assembly, then attach it permanently with glue and screws. As you did when attaching the bottom, drive the screws through the second set of holes in the end cleats.

13

Shim the panels. The thin metal panels will rattle in the ¼"-wide grooves. To prevent this, "shim" the panels from the inside. To do this, simply cut some spacers from scrap wood, 1"-2" long, ⅜" wide, and approximately ³⁄₁₆" thick. (Depending on the thickness of the metal you're using, you may want to adjust the thickness of the shims slightly.) Glue these in place in the grooves, *behind* the panels, on the *inside* of the case and the *backs* of the doors, as shown in the *Metal Panel Joinery Detail.* Use 8-12 shims per panel, to make sure they don't rattle.

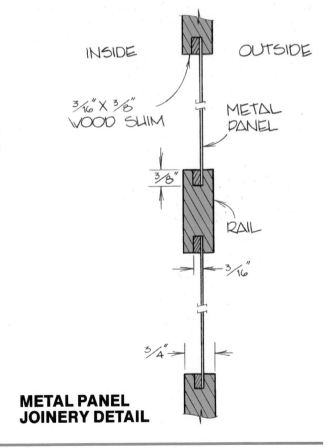

INSIDE OUTSIDE

³⁄₁₆" X ⅜" WOOD SHIM

METAL PANEL

⅜"

RAIL

³⁄₁₆"

¾"

**METAL PANEL
JOINERY DETAIL**

14 **Cut and hang the doors.** Rout a
⅜″-wide, ⅜″-deep rabbet along the edges of
the latch stiles (as opposed to the hinge stiles) of each
door. This rabbet should be on the *front* face of the left
door, and the *back* face of the right door, so that they will
interlock when the doors are closed.

Mortise the opposite door frame stiles and the web
frame stiles for hinges, and attach the doors to the case
with butt hinges. Attach pulls to the doors, and a latch to

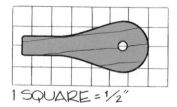

**LATCH
PATTERN**

1 SQUARE = ½″

the top face frame rail, near the middle where it will hold
both doors closed. Use a roundhead screw and a washer
for the latch pivot.

15 **Make and install the drawer.** Cut the
joinery in the drawer parts. As shown in the
Drawer Top View and *Drawer Side View,* the drawer front
and the sides are joined with half-blind dovetails. You can
easily make these joints with a router and a dovetail template. If you don't have a dovetail template, you can substitute a simple rabbet joint, reinforced with screws.

The back fits in dadoes in the sides, and the bottom
in grooves in the inside faces of the front side and back.

Assemble the drawer front, back, and sides with glue, but
let the bottom float in the grooves. After the glue dries,
fit the drawer to the case.

TRY THIS! So that the drawer will slide
smoothly, coat the bottom edge of the sides with
paraffin wax.

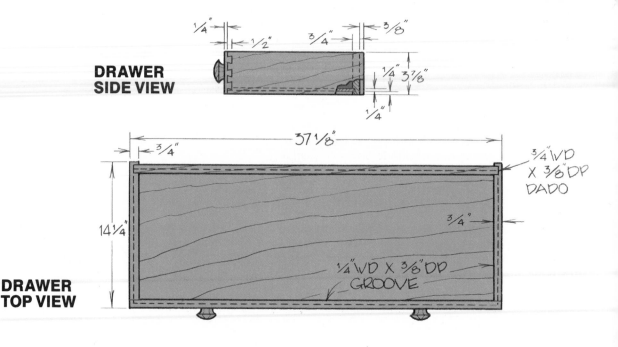

**DRAWER
SIDE VIEW**

**DRAWER
TOP VIEW**

16 **Finish the pie safe.** Remove the doors,
the drawer, and the latch from the case. Mask
off the metal panels — inside and outside — so that you
won't splash finish on them. Finish sand any wooden
parts that may still need it, then apply a finish to the case,
inside and outside. Also, finish the adjustable shelves.

When the finish dries, remove the masking from the
metal panels. Re-install the doors, the drawer, and the
latch. Place shelving supports in the holes in the stiles
where you want to position the adjustable shelves; then
place the shelves on the supports.

Salt Box/ Spoon Rack

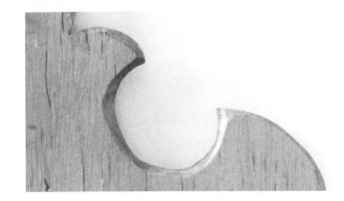

*B*efore the introduction of refined salt, country cooks kept their salt in a wooden "salt box" near the stove. There was a good reason for both the location and the material. Not only was salt convenient — the cook could just reach in the box and "pinch" a little salt to flavor whatever was cooking — the heat from the stove helped keep the salt from clumping, even on humid days. The wood also kept the salt dry; the box absorbed excess moisture from the salt.

Some of the fancier salt boxes had a high back. This back might support small shelves for other spices and condiments, or pegs and brackets on which to hang cooking utensils. The back of this particular salt box has several "spoon racks" to hold cooking or measuring spoons. It's doubtful that you'll use this project for its original purpose, but the box makes a unique country planter for your kitchen or dining room. And you can use the racks to display a spoon collection or to show off your good silverware. ●

Materials List

FINISHED DIMENSIONS

PARTS

A. Back   ½" x 11" x 19½"
B. Bottom   ½" x 6" x 13"
C. Front   ½" x 4" x 12"
D. Sides (2)   ½" x 5¾" x 6"
E. Upper rack   ½" x 2½" x 9"
F. Lower rack   ½" x 3½" x 10"

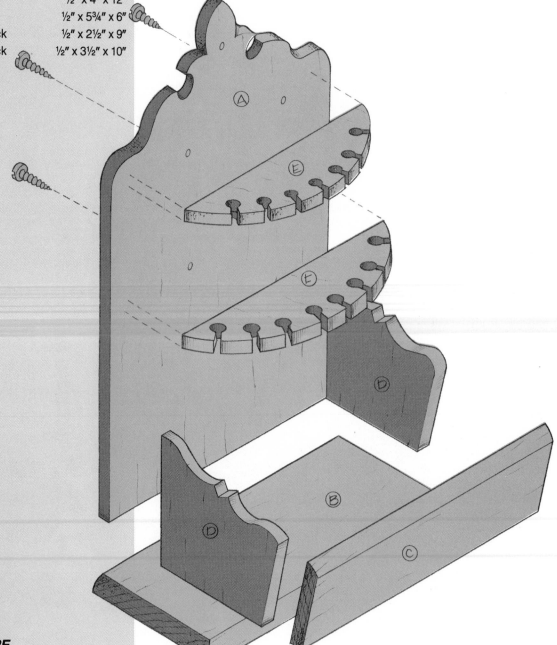

HARDWARE

#8 x ¼" Flathead wood screws (4)
1" Brads (16-20)

1 **Cut the parts to size.** Plane the stock you need to make this project to ½″ thick. If you don't have a planer, you have two options. First of all, there are several woodworking supply houses that sell hardwood stock surfaced to various thicknesses. However, if you don't want to mail-order your wood, you might look around for a lumberyard that does custom millwork, and have them do the planing. When you've gathered the stock you need, cut the parts to the sizes shown in the Materials List. Bevel-rip the bottom edge of the front at 15°.

2 **Cut the shapes of the parts.** Enlarge the *Back Pattern* and *Side Pattern,* then trace the patterns on the stock. With a compass, lay out the racks as shown in the *Upper Rack Layout* and *Lower Rack Layout.* Cut the shapes of the back, sides, and racks with a band saw or scroll saw. Don't cut the notches in the racks just yet; it's easier to make these with the aid of a drill.

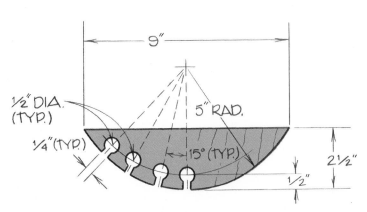

UPPER RACK LAYOUT

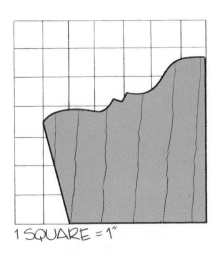

1 SQUARE = 1″

SIDE PATTERN

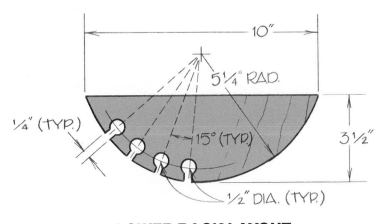

LOWER RACK LAYOUT

1 SQUARE = 1″

BACK PATTERN

3

Cut the notches in the racks. Where you have marked the positions of the notches on the racks, drill ½″-diameter holes through the stock.

Then "open up" these holes with a band saw or scroll saw, cutting ¼″-wide notches from the outside edge of the racks into the holes. (See Figures 1 and 2.)

1/To make the notches in the racks, first drill holes through the stock near the edge of the stock. Back up the work-piece with a scrap of hardwood to reduce the tear-out as the drill exits the wood.

2/With a band saw, cut into the holes from the outside edge of the stock, "opening up" the holes and forming the notches.

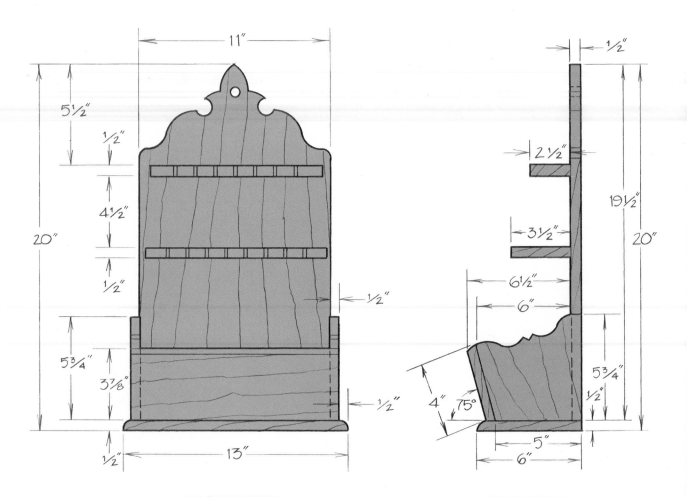

FRONT VIEW   **SIDE VIEW**

4 **Finish sand all parts.**   Sand all the parts smooth, to prepare them for assembly. Remove the saw marks or mill marks from all edges. Be sure to smooth the inside edges of the spoon notches.

5 **Round the edge of the bottom.**   With a quarter-round bit mounted on your shaper or in your router, round over the front and side edges of the bottom.

6 **Assemble the salt box.**   Assemble the parts with glue. Reinforce the racks where they join the back with #8 x 1¼″ flathead wood screws. Reinforce the other joints with brads.

TRY THIS!   To hide the heads of nails, country craftsmen invented "blind nail planes." These are still available from several woodworking supply houses. To use them, first lift a small curl of wood with the plane. *Do not* separate the curl from the stock. Drive a nail where you have lifted the curl and set the head. Put a little glue on the back of the curl and press the curl back into place. Hold the curl down with tape until the glue dries. When you remove the tape, you won't be able to tell there's a nail just under the surface of the wood.

7 **Apply a finish to the salt box.**   Finish sand any portions of the project that still need it. If you wish, "break" the hard edges of the back, racks, and other salt box parts, rounding them over slightly. Then apply a stain or finish to the completed project.

Five-Board Bench

Many pieces of country furniture were made for expediency. The five-board bench is an example of that. Nail together five boards and presto! Instant seating. Holes near the tops of the sides provide handholds, and cutouts in the bottom edges create four feet to keep most of the wooden bench from contacting the damp earth.

However, just because a piece is quick to put together doesn't mean that it can't also be well-made and well-designed. This bench is an exercise in good, economical design and craftsmanship. Although there are only five boards, they are ingeniously arranged so as to brace each other. This keeps the bench stable and upright through all sorts of use and abuse.

A simple project can also be a sight to behold. The flowing shapes and fretwork of the sides and aprons soften what might otherwise be a harsh, utilitarian design and make it pleasing to the eye. The traditional country

"tulip" stencil adds a bit of fancy, to further the effect. All of this makes the five-board bench a truly classic example of country furniture design. ✸

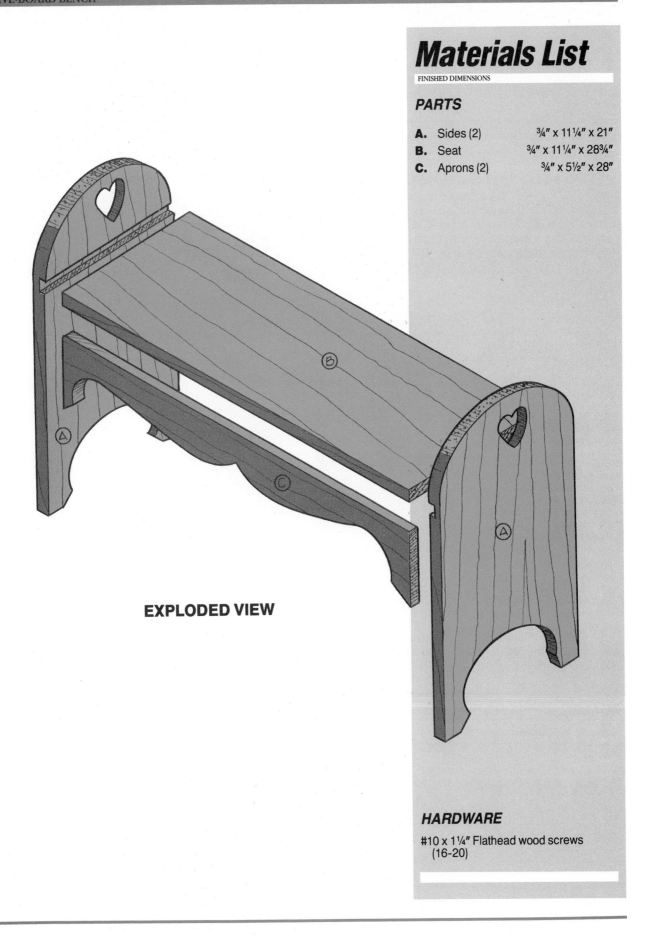

EXPLODED VIEW

Materials List

FINISHED DIMENSIONS

PARTS

A. Sides (2)   ¾" x 11¼" x 21"
B. Seat   ¾" x 11¼" x 28¾"
C. Aprons (2)   ¾" x 5½" x 28"

HARDWARE

#10 x 1¼" Flathead wood screws
  (16-20)

1 Cut the parts to size.

Cut the parts to size. You can make this project from a single 1 x 12, 10′ long. (In fact, you'll have more than a foot left over.) Rip the 5½″-wide stock you need for the aprons, then cut the stock to the lengths shown in the Materials List.

2 Make the seat-to-side joinery.

Make the seat-to-side joinery. Mount a dado cutter in your table saw, and cut two ¾″-wide, ⅜″-deep dadoes in both edges of the back, where shown on the *Front View* and *Side Pattern*. If you don't have a dado cutter, you can use a router and a ¾″-diameter straight bit. If you use the router, make each dado in several passes, routing just ⅛″ deeper with each pass. (See Figure 1.)

1/To rout a dado, clamp a straightedge to the stock to guide the router. To save yourself some time, rout both boards at once. Line them up edge to edge, clamp the straightedge to both of them, and cut the dado.

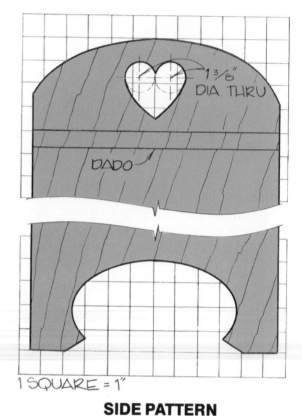

1⅜″ DIA. THRU

DADO

1 SQUARE = 1″

SIDE PATTERN

3 Cut the shapes of the aprons and sides.

Cut the shapes of the aprons and sides. Enlarge the *Side Pattern* and the *Apron Pattern*. Trace these patterns onto the respective boards. With a band saw or a sabre saw, cut the outside shapes of the sides and aprons. Sand away the saw marks from the cut edges.

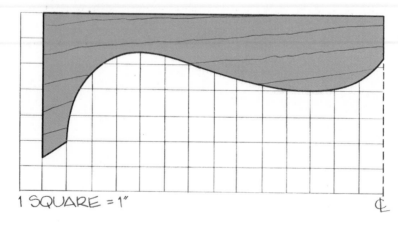

1 SQUARE = 1″

APRON PATTERN

TRY THIS! To save yourself a little work, "pad saw" the shapes of the sides and the aprons. Stack the pieces and nail them together with two or three 3d (1¼"-long) finishing nails or brads to make a "pad." Trace the pattern on the top piece, and cut both pieces at the same time. Leave them tacked together until you've finished all the work you need to do on these pieces, including making the heart-shaped handles and sanding the saw marks.

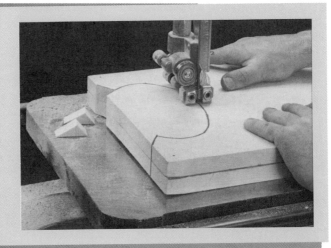

4 Cut out the heart-shaped handles.
Cut the interior shape of the handles in the sides by drilling several holes, then making "piercing cuts" with your sabre saw, jigsaw, or scroll saw. With a holesaw, drill two 1⅜"-diameter holes through the stock to form the top of a heart, as shown in the *Side Pattern*. Insert the saw blade through the holes, then cut down from the holes to remove the waste from the bottom portion of the hearts. (See Figure 2.) Sand the interior cut edges to remove the saw marks.

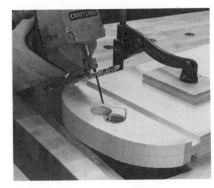

2/When cutting the interior shape of the heart, use a "fine" blade — with 18-20 teeth per inch. The cut edge will be smoother, and you'll have less sanding to do.

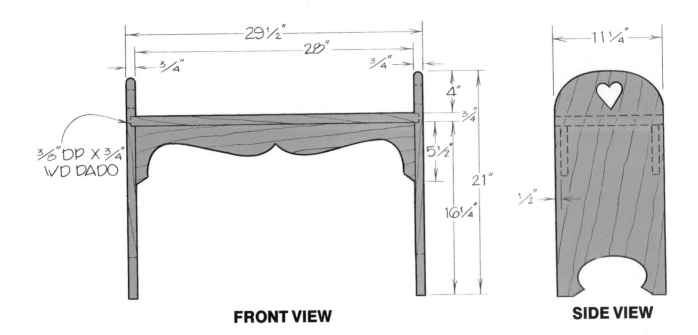

FRONT VIEW

SIDE VIEW

5 Finish sand all parts.

Finish sand all the parts of the bench. Make sure that you remove any remaining saw marks or mill marks. Be careful not to "break" or round over any edges or surface where two parts will be joined.

6 Assemble the bench.

Attach the sides and the seat with glue and screws. Counterbore and countersink the screws so that you can cover the heads with wooden plugs. When the sides and the seat are attached, glue the aprons in place and reinforce the glue joints with screws. Once again, countersink and counterbore the screws. Glue the plugs in place over the screw heads.

TRY THIS! You can easily make your own wooden plugs with a plug cutter. Mount this cutter in your drill press, and cut as many plugs as you need from a scrap of wood. That scrap must match the wood in the project you're building. Cut the plugs free from the scrap with a band saw, then glue them in the counterbored holes. Be careful to line up the grain direction of the plugs so that it's parallel to the grain direction of the surface you're plugging.

7 Finish the bench.

Remove any glue beads and finish sand any parts that may still need it. Sand the wooden plugs flush with the surfaces of the sides and seat. "Break" all the exposed corners, rounding them over with a rasp and sandpaper to give them a soft, used appearance.

Apply a traditional country finish, such as milk paint or an oil finish. If you wish, paint or stencil a design on the ends of the bench. You can use the one we show in the *Stencil Pattern,* or create your own. **Note:** If you finish the bench with milk paint, apply the stencil *after* the paint but *before* the final coat of linseed oil. If you finish the bench with Danish oil or tung oil, apply the stencil to the raw wood before you apply the oil. In both cases, let the stencil dry thoroughly before covering it with the clear finish.

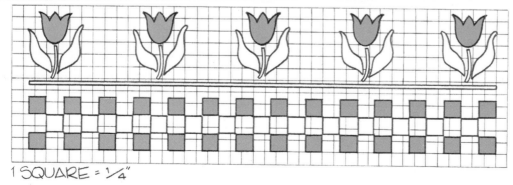

(CUT AS TWO STENCILS USING SHADED AREA AS ONE, AND THE UNSHADED AREA AS THE OTHER.)

STENCIL PATTERN

1 SQUARE = ¼"

Stenciling

Because much country furniture tended to be so plain, country folks invented several different finishing techniques to "dress up" their furniture. Stenciling is one. The craftsman uses a template to paint a simple shape on the wood. This template allows the shape to be repeated over and over again, to form a decorative pattern.

To stencil a country project, you first need to cut a template of the shape or the design you want to reproduce. Consult books on stenciling or folk art to get ideas.

When you've decided on a design, enlarge it or reduce it to the size you want. Then lay a sheet of Mylar or waxed stenciling paper over the design. (Both of these materials are available at art supply stores.) With an *extremely* sharp hobby knife, cut out the design in the template. (See Figure A.) Where necessary to connect interior parts of the design to the exterior shape, leave "bridges" in the template. These bridges give the completed design its characteristic "stenciled" look.

Where different colors butt up against each other, cut separate templates for each color. You can line up two or more templates on the wood by cutting two little triangles near one edge of each template. (See Figure B.) These triangles must be cut in *exactly* the same spot on each template. To do this, it's best to stack the templates up, making sure they are perfectly aligned, then cut the triangles in all the templates at the same time. When you tape the first template to the wood, trace the triangles lightly in pencil. Thereafter, line up each successive template with those triangular marks. After you've finished making the stencil, erase the marks.

Choose the paints for the stencil thoughtfully. Almost any type of paint will do, if you're careful, but quick-drying, thick pigments work the best. Acrylic artist's paints are especially well-suited for wood.

After they dry, they're durable and waterproof. You can also mix up any color you want, using a piece of glass or an old china plate for a palette.

Tape the template to the surface you want to stencil. Dip a stiff brush in the paint and wipe it on the palette so that the brush is fairly "dry." Apply the paint to the wood, brushing in from the border of the opening in the template toward the middle. (See Figure C.) Keep adding coats of paint until the color is thick enough to cover the wood grain or the finish beneath it. Let the paint dry thoroughly, then remove the template.

If you stencil a project that will get a clear finish, apply the stencil first. After a stencil dries, you can usually cover it with oil, varnish, or shellac without discoloring the paint. If you want to stencil a project that will be stained or painted, apply the stain or paint first, then the stencil. Wait for the stain or paint to dry *thoroughly* before you start the stencil.

It's wise to test the stencil paint with the finish that you're going to use *before* you try the combination on the real project. Depending on the stencil paint you use, it may not adhere well to the finish, or the finish may start to dissolve the stencil. If you find this to be a problem, use a different type of paint for the stencil, or a different type of finish for the project.

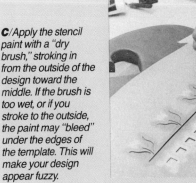

*B/*To help line up successive templates when making a multi-colored stencil, cut triangular shapes near one edge of each one. These triangles must be positioned exactly the same on each template.

*A/*Cut the stencil templates with a sharp hobby knife. Where necessary, leave "bridges" to hold the template together and strengthen the interior parts of the design.

*C/*Apply the stencil paint with a "dry brush," stroking in from the outside of the design toward the middle. If the brush is too wet, or if you stroke to the outside, the paint may "bleed" under the edges of the template. This will make your design appear fuzzy.

Ladder-back Chair

Unlike many country furniture forms that evolved from the joiner's art, the ladder-back chair owes its roots to a completely different woodworking tradition — that of the *turner.* Whereas the joiner worked with boards and beams, the turner's materials were posts and dowels. The joiner assembled his products with square mortises and tenons; the turner used round holes and tenons. The ladder-back chair is a *lathe turning* project. With the exception of the back slats, all the parts — back legs, front legs, rungs, and rails — are made on the lathe.

Ladder-back chairs — so-called because the slats are mortised between the back legs like the rungs of a ladder — were made in Europe long before America was settled. The colonists brought the design with them to New England, but they did not make very many of them; at least, not right away. While the settlers were still struggling to survive, chairs were considered a luxury. Most of our forefathers sat on backless benches. The few chairs that were made were reserved for the elderly, the wealthy, or the very important. (This is where the honorific "Chairman of the Board" comes from.

The chair-man was usually the most important person (or the most well-to-do) at a colonial gathering. The board was the forerunner of the trestle table: a plank laid over two sawbucks.)

When life in the colonies became less precarious, the settlers began to make chairs in quantity. At first, these were copies of European turners' chairs, with elaborately turned legs and rungs. However, decoration soon gave way to practicality. The project you see here is a typical American country ladder-back design, all business with just a minimum of decoration. This particular ladder-back chair was made in the Shaker community of Mount Lebanon, New York, during the early part of the nineteenth century.

Despite its simple appearance, the chair is actually a sophisticated woodworking design. Early on, country craftsmen found that they couldn't rely on glue to hold their chairs together. Because the wooden members of a turned chair are fairly delicate, the wood flexes every time someone sits down in the chair. Sooner or later most of the glue joints pop. Instead, these chairs are held together by the tightly woven seat and two small pegs on either end of the top slat.

Materials List

FINISHED DIMENSIONS

PARTS

A. Back legs (2)   1⅜" dia. x 41¼"

B. Front legs (2)   1⅜" dia. x 18¼"

C. Front stretcher
and rungs (3)   ¾" dia. x 17½"

D. Back stretcher
and rungs (2)   ¾" dia. x 13⅛"

E. Side stretchers
and rungs (6)   ¾" dia. x 13¼"

F. Back slats (3)   ¼" x 2¾" x 13½"

G. Pegs (2)   ¼" dia. x 1"

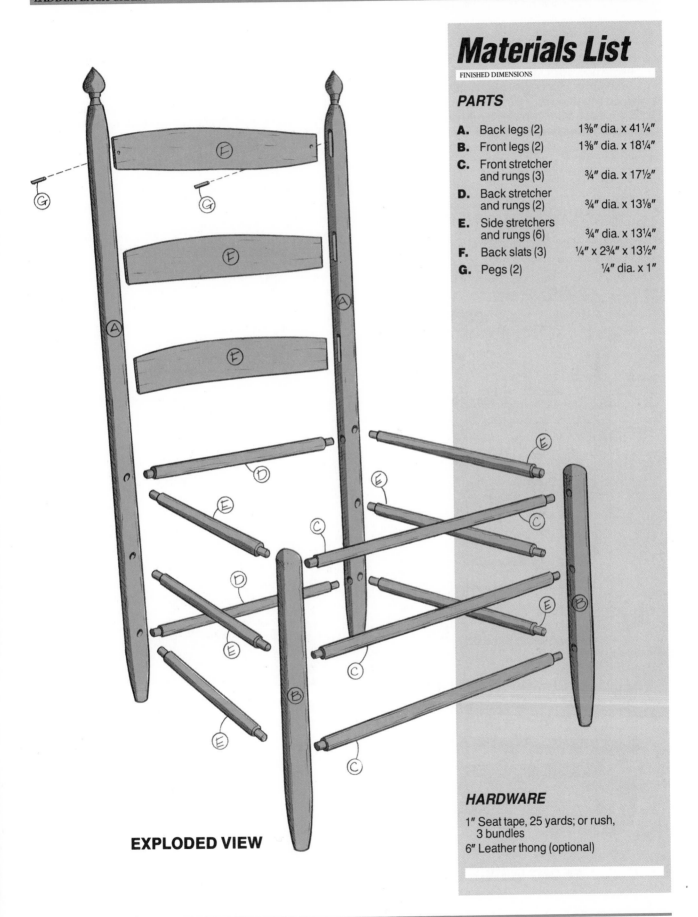

EXPLODED VIEW

HARDWARE

1" Seat tape, 25 yards; or rush,
3 bundles

6" Leather thong (optional)

1

Cut all parts to size. Select clear, straight hardwood stock for this project. Stock with knots, burls and other defects may split on the lathe or give way when you sit on the chair. Traditionally, ladder-back chairs are made from maple or birch. However, you can also use cherry, walnut, oak, or hickory.

Cut the round parts slightly larger than what is shown in the Materials List. Since all these parts are turned on the lathe, you want to make the stock ¼"-½" wider and thicker, and 2"-3" longer than the finished dimensions. Cut the slats 4"-6" longer than needed. You'll need this extra length to help bend these parts.

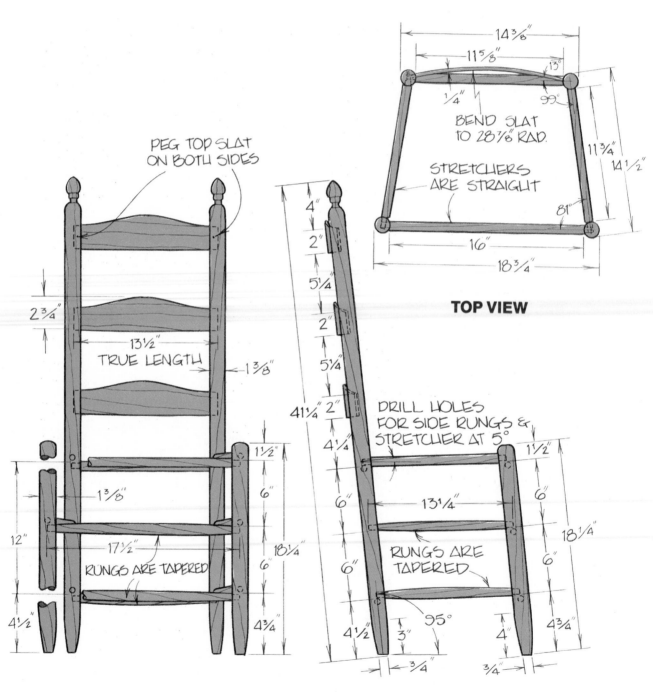

TOP VIEW

FRONT VIEW

SIDE VIEW

2 *Turn the legs, rungs, and stretchers.*

Since all these parts have very little decoration, the turning is straightforward. The only beads and coves you have to turn are on the pommels in the ends of the back legs. These aren't critical to the design; you can eliminate them or change them to suit your own tastes.

The round tenons on the ends of the rungs and stretchers are, however, critical to the design. These tenons (and their shoulders) add strength and stability to the chair frame. Turn the tenons carefully, working with a tenon gauge that you can make yourself. For complete instructions on how to make and use a turning gauge, see "Step by Step: Turning to a Specific Diameter" elsewhere in this book. Make the gauge as shown, but change the dimensions of the slot and the hole to gauge the tenons you want to turn — ½″ in diameter. Turn the tenon until the gauge slips over it up to the step. Then *sand* the tenon until the gauge slips over the tenon com-

1/Make a tenon gauge from a piece of scrap wood to accurately gauge the diameter of the tenons as you turn them. Turn the tenon until the gauge slips over it up to the step. Then sand the tenon, until the gauge slips over it completely.

pletely. (See Figure 1.) When this happens, stop sanding immediately — the tenon is at the proper diameter.

You'll also have to turn curved or "bellied" tapers in *some* of the parts. The rungs are slightly fatter in the middle than at the ends, while the stretchers are straight. The legs are mostly straight, but there is a slight taper in the bottom 3″-4″, as shown in the *Front View* and *Side View*.

TRY THIS! All of the parts are fairly slender — the largest finished diameter is just 1⅜″. Because of this, you want to be careful that the spindles don't "whip" or bow on the lathe. Use just enough pressure between the centers to keep the stock firmly mounted in the lathe. When turning the longer pieces, use a steadyrest to keep them from whipping. Some manufacturers offer these as accessories, or you can make your own following the plans shown here.

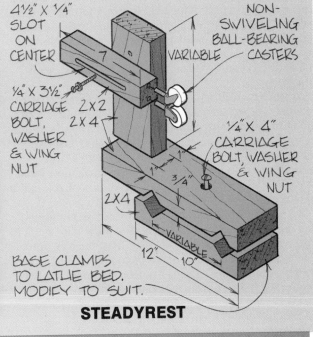

STEADYREST

4½″ X ¼″ SLOT ON CENTER

¼″ X 3½″ CARRIAGE BOLT, WASHER & WING NUT

2 X 2
2 X 4

NON-SWIVELING BALL-BEARING CASTERS

VARIABLE

¼″ X 4″ CARRIAGE BOLT, WASHER & WING NUT

1″
1″
¾″

2 X 4

VARIABLE

12″   10″

BASE CLAMPS TO LATHE BED. MODIFY TO SUIT.

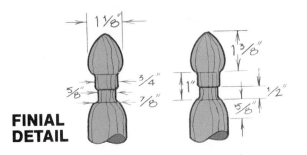

FINIAL DETAIL

1⅛″
1⅜″
¾″
1″
⅝″
⅞″
½″
⅝″

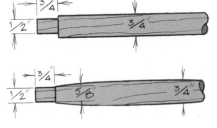

¾″
¾″
½″

STRETCHER (MAKE 4)

¾″
⅝″   ¾″
½″

TAPERED RUNGS (MAKE 7)

3 If necessary, use a "dowel maker" to shape the back legs.

If you have an ordinary lathe, you may have some trouble turning the back legs. Most home workshop lathes have a throw of 36", not long enough to accommodate the legs. You'll either have to find a lathe with a longer throw or use an old-time "dowel maker" to shape these parts. These are also called "rounding planes" or, simply, "rounders." (See Figure 2.) You can make one from scrap wood and an old plane iron.

In the middle of the face of a 2" x 4" x 17" block of hardwood, scribe a circle 1¾" in diameter. Then drill a 1⅜"-diameter hole inside this circle, through the block, using the same centerpoint. This hole is the same size as the leg you want to make — 1⅜" in diameter. Using a gouge, enlarge the hole in the front of the block so that it tapers ⅜" from front to back. The opening in the front should be 1¾" in diameter (the size of the circle you scribed); in back, 1⅜" in diameter, as shown in the *Dowel Maker Cross Section*.

On the front of the block, draw a line parallel to the top edge and tangent to the enlarged hole. Then make a second line so that it intersects the circumference of the hole at the tangent, 45° to the tangent line. Draw a third line from the center of the hole so that it intersects the second line at 90°. (See Figure 3.) Cut along the second and third line with your band saw, to open up a slot in the dowel maker. The second line should be cut with the table tilted at approximately 10° to match the taper of the hole.

If you have a lathe, mount the dowel maker between the centers and turn the handles. If you don't have a lathe you can saw the shapes of the handles on a band saw and round them with a rasp. Secure a plane iron or spokeshave knife to the tilted face of the slot with a large roundhead wood screw. Test the dowel maker on some scraps and adjust the position of the knife so that it cuts a dowel precisely the diameter of the back leg.

Use the dowel maker in the same manner as a threading die. First, knock off the corners of the square stock to make the wood roughly octagonal. Twist the tool onto the wood, pushing down gently as you turn. The blade will shave the stock, leaving a perfectly formed leg. (See Figure 4.) It won't make the pommels, however. You'll need to carve these by hand, or turn them as separate pieces and dowel them to the legs. Smooth and taper the legs with a spokeshave.

2/If your lathe doesn't have a long enough throw to turn the back legs, you can also use a "dowel maker." Make this tool from a scrap of hardwood and an old plane iron.

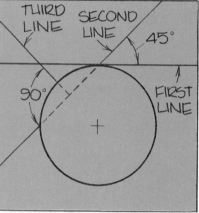

3/To mark the slot in the dowel maker, draw three lines on the front as shown here. Cut along the second and third line. The second line should be cut on a bevel of 10° to match the taper of the hole in the dowel maker.

4/Use the dowel maker as you would a threading die. Twist the tool onto the stock, pressing down gently as you turn. To make it easier to round the stock with the dowel maker, you may want to knock off the corners, making it roughly octagonal.

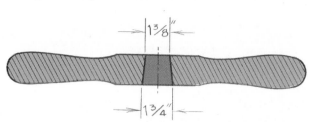

CROSS-SECTION OF DOWEL MAKER

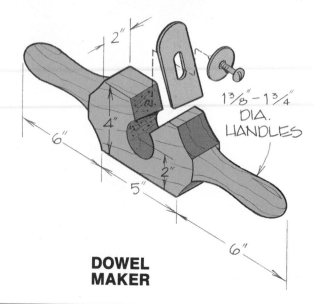

DOWEL MAKER

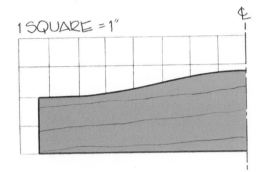

1 SQUARE = 1"

BACK SLAT PATTERN

4 **Bend the slats.** The slats of ladder-back chairs are bowed slightly to fit your back. These parts are thin enough (¼″) that you can do this bending easily in a home workshop, without making an expensive steamer. There are two methods you can use.

The first requires a woodstove. Cut the shapes of the slats on a band saw and soak them in water overnight. The next day, light a fire in your stove and press a wet slat against the hot stovepipe. Hold the slat by the ends, press forward gently, and rock the wood back and forth to heat it evenly. Be careful that it doesn't char! As the stock heats up, you'll feel the wood "give." Keep pressing forward until you have the curve you want. Let the wood cool and cut off the slat to the proper length.

If you don't have a woodstove — or if it's summer-time, and you don't want to light a fire — boil the slats in a roasting pan for 45-60 minutes, then place them in a bending jig — you can bend all three at once. Clamp the part of the jig together so that the slats are bent. (See Figure 5.) Let them dry at least two weeks in the bending

jig. There may be some "springback" when you remove the clamps, but this is normal. Depending on the wood you use and how it's seasoned, boiled or steamed, wood will lose up to 20% of its curve when it comes out of a bending jig. Compensate for this by making the curve of the jig slightly more pronounced than the final curve of the slat.

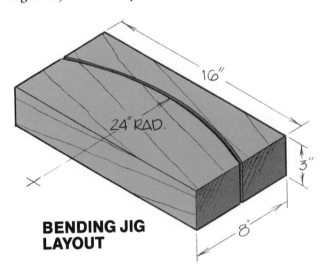

16"

24″ RAD.

3"

8"

BENDING JIG LAYOUT

5/To bend the slats, boil them in a roasting pan, then clamp them in a bending jig and let them dry for at least two weeks.

5 **Make the mortises in the legs.** The mortises — holes and slots — in the front and back legs must line up properly with each other. There are two "lines" of these holes as you sight down the front legs (for front rungs/stretcher and side rungs/stretchers), and three lines in the back legs (for side rungs/stretchers, back rung/stretcher, and slats.) Each line of holes or slots must be properly drilled or cut at the proper angle to the other lines, as shown in the *Top View.* It's easy to mark these angles on the ends of the legs. But how do you transfer these marks down the length of the stock, so that you can keep all the mortises in the same line? The simplest way is with a long V-shaped jig. Rest the stock in the jig and use one side of the "V" as a straightedge. (See Figure 6.)

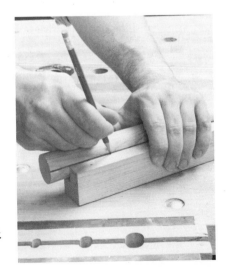

6/To help mark the positions of the mortises in the front and back legs, make a V-jig out of 1 x 2 stock. Use one side of the jig as a straightedge.

This V-jig also comes in handy when it's time to drill the holes or cut the slots. Secure the leg in the jig with metal straps and wood screws to keep the stock properly aligned to the bit or cutter. When cutting the slots, clamp a fence to the worktable to guide the jig. (See Figure 7.)

Make the holes on a drill press, and cut the slots on an overarm router. Remember that the holes for the side rungs and stretchers are drilled 5° off square, as shown in the *Side View.*

7/*You can also use this V-jig to hold the legs while you drill or rout the mortises. Clamp the leg in the jig with metal strap and screws. Use a piece of leather to keep the strap from scratching the leg stock.*

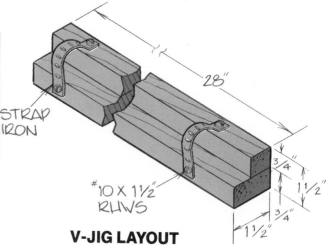

STRAP IRON

#10 X 1½″ RHWS

28″

3/4″

1½″

3/4″

1½″

V-JIG LAYOUT

TRY THIS!   If you don't have an overarm router, you can use a drill press for making the slots, provided you take certain precautions when routing the slots. An ordinary drill chuck doesn't properly support the shank of a router bit against sideways thrust, and the bit may bend or break. To prevent this, make a collet from an ¼″ I.D. bushing. Cut a slot down one side of the bushing with a hacksaw. Mount the router bit in the collet, and clamp the collet in the drill chuck.

6 **Assemble the chair frame.**   Finish sand all parts, and dry assemble the chair frame to test the fit. If you're satisfied that all parts fit properly, reassemble the chair frame with glue. However, don't depend on glue to hold the chair together. The parts of the frame flex every time you sit in it, and many of the glue joints will eventually pop. Traditionally, ladder-back chairs are held together by tightly-woven seats and a few well-placed pegs.

Peg the top slats to the back posts. Drill the peg holes from the back, and stop the holes before they go through the front. On some ladder-back chairs, all the slats are pegged, but this isn't necessary.

7 **Apply a finish to the chair.**   You'll want to finish your chair *before* you weave the seat; it's extremely hard to apply the finish after the chair seat has been completed. Country craftsmen used a variety of finishes and stains. Two of the most common were a simple oil finish and milk paint.

8

Weave a seat. There are many, many different options for weaving a seat. Ladder-back chairs have been covered with cloth tape, rush, splint, woven straw, cane, leather, and even twisted paper. We'll show you two of the most common options: tape and rush.

Cloth tape — Cloth tape seats were developed by the Shakers in the late 1830s. This tape, or "listing," is woven onto the chair frames in simple patterns. Most tape seats are woven with two colors — a light and a dark — to make a checkerboard or herringbone design. Select the colors of tapes you'll use for the *warps* (front-to-back tape) and the *wefts* (side-to-side tape). Traditionally, the darker tape was used for the warps, so that the finished seat wouldn't show the dirt where your legs rubbed against it.

Begin weaving with the warps. Tack the lead end of a coil of tape to the back stretcher, near a back leg. (See Figure 8.) Bring the coil over the back stretcher to the front stretcher, over and under the front stretcher, then back under and over the back stretcher. Do not twist the tape; keep it stretched as tightly as possible. (See Figure 9.) Keep the warps square to the front and back stretchers. Since the seat frame is not square, but slightly trapezoid-shaped, you'll have to leave two small triangular areas open on either side of the seat. (Don't worry — you'll fill these in later.) If you need to sew two coils of

tape together, make the seam on a *bottom* warp, so that it won't show. When you finish wrapping the last warp, cut off the tape. Lap the tail end of the tape over the last warp, and tack it to the back stretcher.

Before you begin the wefts, stuff a ¾″-thick foam rubber pad in between the top and bottom wraps. This will make the cloth tape seat more comfortable. When the pad is in place, tack the lead end of a weft coil to a side stretcher, close to the back leg. Wrap the wefts onto the side stretchers in the same manner as you wrapped the warps, but weave the wefts in between the warps. (See Figure 10.) If you weave over-one and under-one, the tapes will form a checkerboard design. If you weave over-two and under-two, skipping *one* at the beginning of each weft row, you'll make a herringbone pattern. (See Figure 11.) Where the warp tape is overlapped (on the last bottom warp), treat the two overlapping tapes as a single tape when weaving in the wefts. If you don't, the design won't be the same on both the top and bottom of the seat.

Finish the cloth tape seat by filling in the triangular areas on either side of the seat with additional strips of warp tape. Glue the ends of these strips to the undersides of the wefts, or pull the wefts aside and tack them to the side stretchers. (See Figure 12.) Slide the wefts back in place to cover the tacks.

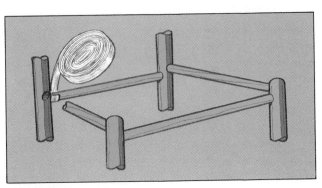

8/Tack the cloth tape to the back seat stretcher, near the back leg.

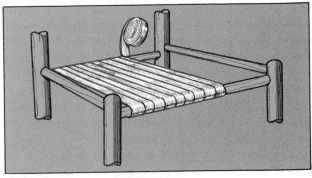

9/Wind the warp tape over and under the front stretcher, then under and over the back stretcher. Continue until you

have filled in the entire seat, except for two small triangular areas on either side. Do not twist the tape.

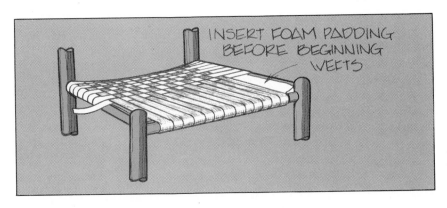

INSERT FOAM PADDING BEFORE BEGINNING WEFTS

10/Insert foam padding between the top and bottom warps, then weave the wefts onto the seat.

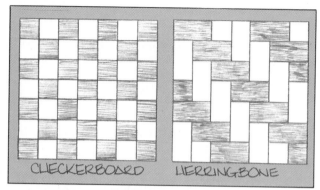

11/As you weave the wefts, you can make two simple patterns — a checkerboard (over-one and under-one) or a herringbone (over-two and under-two).

To make the herringbone, you have to skip one at the beginning of each new weft row.

12/Finish weaving the tape seat by filling in the triangular areas with short warps. Pull back the weft tapes and tack the ends of the warp tapes to the side stretchers.

Rush — To weave a seat from rush, first soak the rush bundles in water overnight. The rush needs to be wet for two reasons: First, the rush is very brittle and may break if it's not wetted. Secondly, the wet rush will shrink as it dries, tightening the woven seat.

The rush is woven onto the seat so that the warps (front-to-back strands) and wefts (side-to-side strands) are square to each other. However, the seat frame, when viewed from the top is not square, but slightly trapezoid shaped. To keep the warps and wefts square, begin your weaving by filling in two small triangular areas (one on either side of the seat) with rush. Tie the end of a strand of rush to a side stretcher near the left front leg. Bring that strand over and around the front stretcher, over and

around the side stretcher, then across to the other side of the seat frame. Repeat the weave: Wind the strand over and around the side stretcher, over and around the front stretcher, then tie the strand to the side stretcher near the right front leg. (See Figure 13.) Tie another strand to the left side stretcher, a little further away from the front leg than the first strand. Weave the strand onto the frame as before. Continue until you have filled in the triangular places.

When the triangles are filled in and you can tie a strand to the side stretcher near the *back* leg, start to fill in the entire seat. Wind the rush around the stretchers at each corner in turn: left-front, right-front, right-back, left-back, and so on. (See Figure 14.) You should be able to weave

13/Begin weaving a rush seat by filling in the triangles. Tie the ends of the first rush strand to the side stretchers near the front legs. Tie each succeeding strand farther back on the stretchers, progressively closer to the back legs.

14/When the triangles are filled in, weave the remaining rectangular space with one long strand. Starting at the front left corner, wrap the strand over and under the front stretcher, then over and under the left side stretcher. Bring the strand across to the right front corner, and wrap it over and under the right side stretcher, then over and under the front stretcher. Continue on to the back right corner, then the back left corner. Repeat until the entire seat is covered with rush.

the rest of the seat with a single strand of rush. If you do have to splice the rush, make the splices on a *bottom* warp or weft (so that it won't show), as far away from a stretcher as possible (so that it won't make a lump. To make the splice, "whip" the ends of the strands together with string, winding the string round and round the rush. (See Figure 15.)

As you weave, you may want to "pad" the rush. This make the weave tighter and the seat more comfortable. Every ten turns around the seat, stuff a little cotton batting into the "pockets" formed by the woven rush at the corners. (See Figure 16.) Use a small stick to pack the batting in between the rush.

Because of the way the seat is proportioned, you'll fill in the wefts before you finish the warps. When you have no more room on the side stretchers for wefts, weave the rush front-to-back — over and under the front stretcher, then over and under the back stretcher. (See Figure 17.) Continue until the entire seat is filled in. End the weave on the bottom of the seat, and tie off the end of the rush to a warp strand on either side. Use the same method you used for splicing the rush — whip the strands together with string.

Wet the entire seat with a damp rag and let it dry thoroughly. There is no need to finish the rush, although some craftsmen prefer to apply a coat of clear shellac or varnish.

Here are two sources for cloth tape and rush:

Shaker Workshops
P.O. Box 1028
Concord, MA 01742

Connecticut Cane and Reed Company
P.O. Box 1276
Manchester, CT 06040

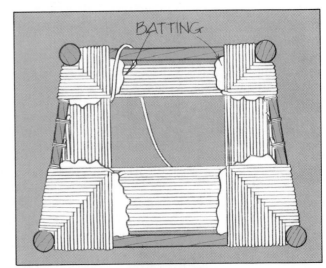

16/If you wish, pad the rush to make the seat more comfortable. Every ten turns around the seat, stop weaving and stuff cotton batting into the "pockets" formed by the rush at the corners. Use a small stick to pack the batting in between the rush.

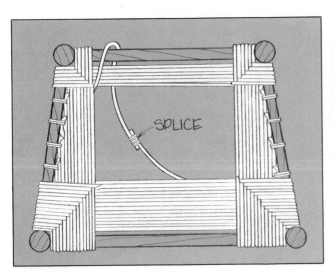

15/To splice two strands of rush, "whip" the ends together with string. Make these splices on the bottom of the chair seat, where they won't show.

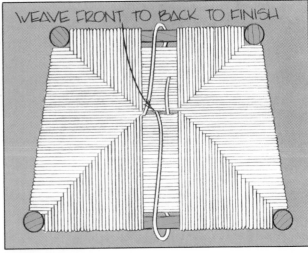

17/When the side stretchers have been filled by wefts, weave the rush front-to-back, filling in the rest of the warps on the front and back stretchers.

Dough Box

Before the advent of store-bought bread, the country cook baked almost every day. Bread was perhaps the most important staple in the country diet, and fresh bread was the sign of a well-run kitchen. Consequently, the utensils used to make bread were extremely important to the country kitchen. One of those utensils was the "dough box."

The dough box was actually a small wooden trough or bin on legs. The trough was used to knead the bread dough, then covered so that the bread could rise undisturbed.

Like many pieces of country furniture, it was expected to do double duty, so it was used as an extra work table while the bread was rising, or when the basin was not in use. The top was hinged in the middle so that the cook could easily check on the dough while it was rising, and it was left unattached so that she could remove the top completely when it was time to knead the dough or take it out of the trough and put it in the oven.

Today, few dough boxes are used for their original purposes. But they can still do double duty. Around the home, they make a unique end table or provide extra counter space. The bin can be used to store table linens, kitchen appliances, or cooking utensils. The one you see here is used to hold recipes and sewing patterns. ✹

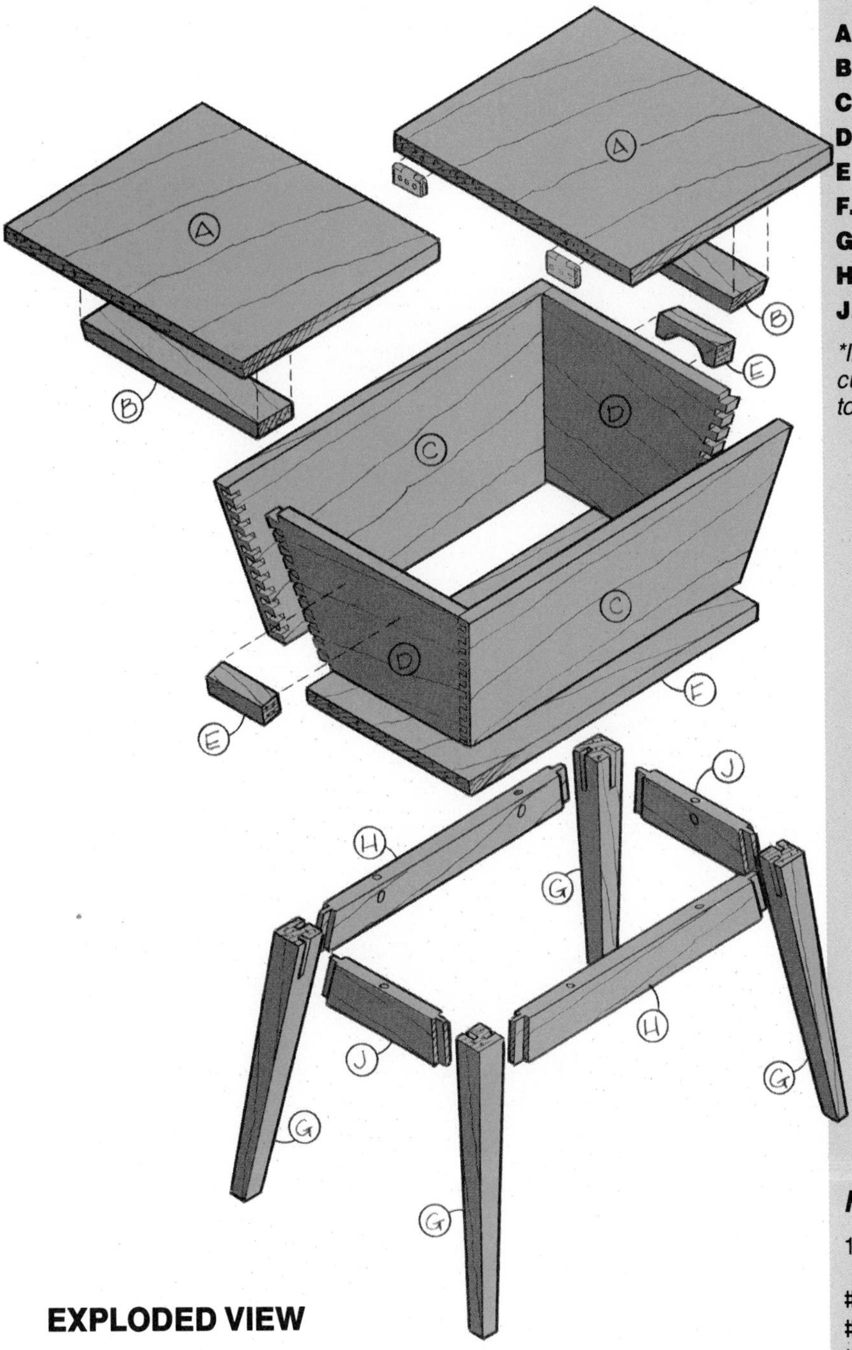

Materials List

FINISHED DIMENSIONS

PARTS

A.	Lids (2)	¾" x 14½" x 17"
B.	Lid Cleats (2)	¾" x 2½" x 13"
C.	Sides (2)	¾" x 9¾" x 23¾"
D.	Ends (2)	¾" x 9¾" x 13"*
E.	Handles (2)	1" x 1¼" x 4"
F.	Bottom	¾" x 11½" x 20¾"
G.	Legs (4)	1¾" x 1¾" x 16¼"
H.	Side aprons (2)	¾" x 2½" x 17¾"
J.	End aprons (2)	¾" x 2½" x 8½"

Increase this dimension to 13¾" if you cut the optional half-blind dovetails, and to 14½" if you make full dovetails.

EXPLODED VIEW

HARDWARE

1½" x 2½" Brass butt hinges and
   mounting screws
#12 x 1¾" Flathead wood screws (4)
#10 x 1¼" Roundhead wood screws (6)
10 x 1¼" Flathead wood screws (12)
#8 x 1¼" Flathead wood screws (12)
   — optional*

Use instead of dovetail to assemble sides and ends.

1

Cut all the parts to size.   Glue up the wide stock you need for the lids and bottom. Then cut all the parts to the sizes shown on the Materials List. Cut the legs, sides, ends, and aprons ½″-1″ larger than the dimensions given, so that you have room to make the miter and bevel cuts required.

CUTTING CORNERS FOR COMPOUND ANGLES OF BOX SIDES & ENDS

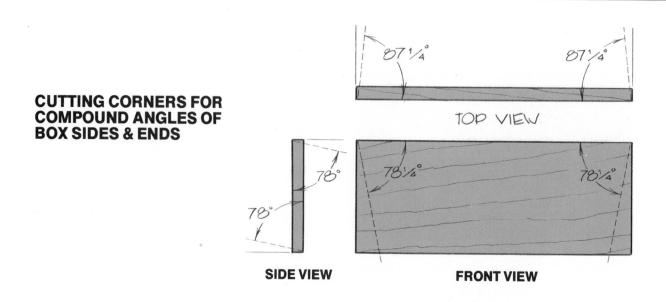

TOP VIEW

SIDE VIEW   FRONT VIEW

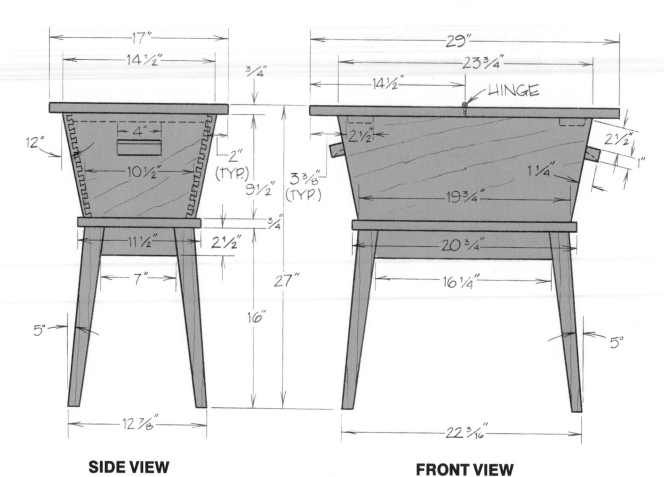

SIDE VIEW   **FRONT VIEW**

2 Miter and bevel the sides and ends.

Bevel-rip the tops and bottom edges of the sides and ends at 12°. Then compound-miter the adjoining edges, with the bevel angle at 2¾° and the miter angle at 78¼°.

Important note: The compound-miter angles given here are straight from a chart, and should be considered as "ballpark" angles only. Setting a saw angle to ¼° increments is almost impossible; moreover, every saw is a little different, and depending on the alignment of the arbor, blade, and worktable, the angles may or may not be correct for *that* saw. We suggest you first cut half-size sides and ends from scrap wood and put them together to check the angles. If they don't quite fit, make small adjustments until they do. When you get the angles just right, cut the ends and sides from good stock.

3 Join the ends and sides with dovetails (optional).

As we show in the *Dovetail Detail* and other working drawings, the ends and sides can be joined by either full or half-blind dovetails. These are optional; you can also use ordinary butt joints, reinforced with dowels or screws. If you elect to make the dovetails, they can be easily cut with your router and a dovetail template. They can also be made by hand, of course. However, hand-cutting angled dovetails requires a great deal of complex calculating, sawing, and chiseling. If you have the skills, then by all means, do it by hand. But for simplicity's sake, we'll cover just the router techniques.

First, you have to adapt your template to hold the pieces at the proper angles while you're routing the dovetails. To do this, cut a pair of hardwood wedges. Each wedge should be as long as the template, and 2½" to 3" wide. One face of each wedge must be beveled at 87¼° — the same angle as the beveled ends of the sides and ends. Insert the pair of wedges — beveled faces together —between the surface of the template and the clamp that holds the "tail" stock to the template. (See Figure 1.) When the end pieces — the pieces in which the tails are cut — are inserted between the beveled faces, the wedges and the clamp will hold this tail stock at the proper angle to the sides or "pin" stock.

Mark the insides of the sides and ends. Secure a side and an end to the template so that the inside surfaces are facing up and out. The compound-mitered edges must butt up against one another, with the side clamped flat to rout pins and the end clamped at a slight angle (between the wedges) to rout tails. With the parts clamped so, position the routing guide on top of them.

Rout the dovetail as you would normally, following the guide. Repeat this procedure for each corner, routing half-blind dovetails to join the sides and ends. (See Figure 2.)

Important note: It's impossible to give specific instructions for positioning the parts and the dovetail template on the jig, since these will change slightly with the manufacturer of the template. Consult your owner's manual, and make several "scrap" sides and ends so that you can experiment with the jig before you rout the "good" parts.

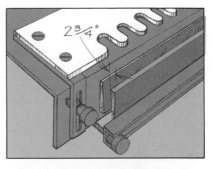

1/To hold the workpieces at the proper angles to each other when you rout the dovetails, make a pair of hardwood wedges. These wedges fit between the surface of the template and the clamp that holds the stock in which the tails will be cut.

2/With the compound-mitered ends of the pieces butting up against one another in the template, rout the dovetails as you would normally. Because of the angles involved, it may take some experimentation to make the fine adjustments needed. Practice on scrap wood before you cut good stock.

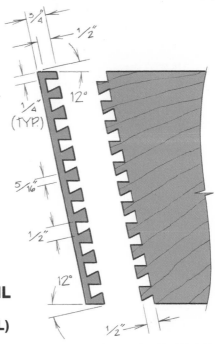

DOVETAIL DETAIL (OPTIONAL)

4 Miter and bevel the aprons and legs.

Bevel the top and bottom edges of the aprons at 5°, and miter the ends at 85°. Compound-miter the top and bottom ends of the legs, with the bevel angle at 4¾°, and the miter angle at 85¼°. Remember that the ends of the legs must be cut parallel to each other, as shown in the *Leg Layout*.

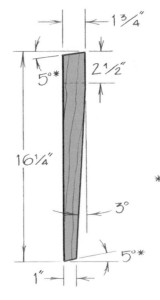

LEG LAYOUT

1¾"
5°*
2½"
16¼"
3°
5°*
1"

*NOTE: ENDS OF LEGS ARE COMPOUND-MITERED AT 4¾° AND 85¼°. THIS PRODUCES A TILT OF 5°.

5 Join the legs and aprons with slot mortises and tenons.

With a router, cut ¼"-wide, ¾"-deep, 2½"-long slot mortises in the inside surfaces of the legs, near the top end. (See Figure 3.) With a dado cutter, make matching tenons in the ends of the aprons. These tenons must be cut at 85°, so that the shoulders are parallel to the mitered ends of the stock. Round the bottom edge of the tenon, so that its shape matches the mortise. (See Figure 4.)

3/Use a router and a straight bit to make the slot mortises. This step is a lot easier if you have a "router table" accessory for your router. Use a fence to guide the work, and a stop block to stop the mortise when it's 2½" long.

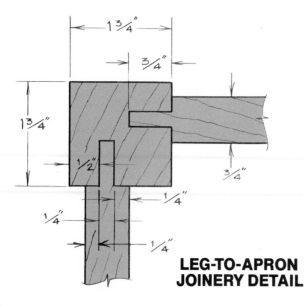

1¾"
¾"
1¾"
½"
¾"
¼"
¼"
¼"

LEG-TO-APRON JOINERY DETAIL

4/Using a chisel and a rasp, round over the bottom edges of the tenons to fit the mortises.

6

Taper the legs. Taper-cut the *inside* faces of the legs, so that each leg tapers from 1¾" square at the top to 1" square at the bottom. Use a tapering jig to hold the legs at a slight angle to the table saw blade while you cut. (See Figure 5.) Start each taper cut 2½" from the top of the leg, as shown in the *Leg Layout*.

5/Cut the tapers in the legs, using a tapering jig to hold the legs at the proper angle to the blade. Start the taper cuts 2½" from the top ends of the legs, and cut only the inside faces of the legs.

7

Drill screw pockets in the aprons. The leg-and-apron assembly is attached to the dough box assembly with screws. These screws are hidden in "screw pockets" in the inside faces of the aprons. Screw pockets are best made on a drill press. First, drill a ½"-diameter counterbore hole at a 15° angle in the inside face of the stock. Stop the hole approximately ⅜" before you reach the edge. Then drill a ³⁄₁₆" pilot hole, centered in the larger hole, through to the edge of the stock. (See Figure 6 and the *Screw Pocket Detail*.) The pilot hole should be approximately centered in the edge, where it exits the stock.

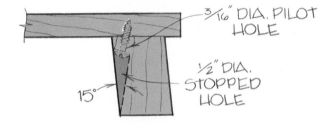

³⁄₁₆" DIA. PILOT HOLE

½" DIA. STOPPED HOLE

15°

SCREW POCKET DETAIL

6/To attach the leg-and-apron assembly to the dough box, drill screw pockets in the aprons. Both the counterbore holes and the pilot holes of these screw pockets should be drilled at a 15° angle in the stock.

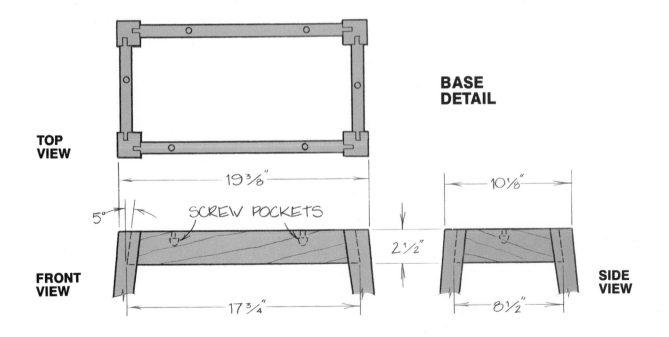

BASE DETAIL

TOP VIEW

19⅜"

10⅛"

5°

SCREW POCKETS

2½"

FRONT VIEW

17¾"

8½"

SIDE VIEW

8 **Carve the handles.** Clamp the handle stock in a vise and carve recesses in the back, bottom corners with a gouge chisel. (See Figure 7.) Make each

recess ½″ deep and 1″ wide, as shown in the *Handle Details.* Smooth the surfaces of the completed recesses with sandpaper.

7/Using a gouge chisel, carve recesses in the bottom, back corners of the handles. Smooth the recesses with sandpaper, after you've carved them.

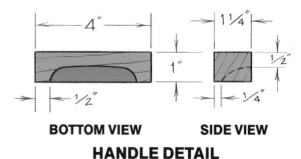

BOTTOM VIEW   **SIDE VIEW**

HANDLE DETAIL

9 **Join the lids with hinges.** Mortise the inside edges of the lids for the butt hinges. Install

the hinges in the lids with the pins *up.* If the pins face down, the lids won't open properly.

10 **Finish sand all the parts.** Scrape and sand all the parts you have made. Be careful not to round over or "break" the corners as you sand. Usually,

you want to wait until *after* you assemble a project to break the corner. This way, the completed project takes on a naturally worn look.

11 **Assemble the dough box.** Assemble the legs and the aprons with glue. If you wish, reinforce the mortise-and-tenon joints with ¼″-diameter pegs.

Assemble the sides and ends with glue. Reinforce these glue joints with #8 flathead screws, if you have decided not to make dovetails. Counterbore and countersink the screws, then cover the screw heads with wooden plugs.

Glue the handles to the ends of the dough box, and reinforce the joints with #12 flathead screws. Drive the screws from the inside of the box, through the ends and into the handles.

Using #10 flathead screws, attach the cleats to the lid assembly, and the bottom to the dough box assembly. *Do*

not glue these parts in place. Instead drill slightly oversized pilot holes for the screws. This will allow the wide wooden parts to expand and contract with changes in humidity, without being restricted by the adjoining parts. If you use glue or make the screws too tight, the completed dough box will warp or split out.

Attach the leg-and-apron assembly to the bottom of the dough box with #10 roundhead screws and washers. Drive these screws through the screw pockets in the aprons. Once again, *do not* glue this assembly in place.

Important note: *Do not* attach the lid assembly to the dough box. Traditionally, this was just laid in place; the cleats kept it from sliding around. With the lid unattached, you can access the inside of the box from either end.

12 **Finish the dough box.** Remove the lid from the dough box and remove the hinges. Finish-sand any parts that still need it, and round over or break the hard corners. Apply a stain

or finish, being careful to evenly coat *all* the surfaces, even those that won't show. This will help to keep the parts from warping or distorting. When the finish dries, reassemble the lid and put it back in place.

Dry Sink

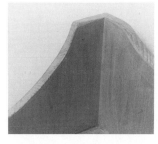

Dry sink" is a modern term, invented sometime after indoor plumbing became common, to describe a sink without plumbing. The old country name for this particular piece of furniture was a "bucket bench." It was so-called because it developed from a simple bench.

The earliest settlers used to keep a low bench outside the door of their cabin to hold buckets of water for drinking, washing, and dousing the fire. When they could afford the time and materials to build something more sophisticated, they raised the bench so that it made a countertop for washing and added a shelf beneath the top to store extra buckets of water. Still later, they moved the bench indoors for convenience. To keep water from slopping on the cabin floor, the settlers attached splashguards around the countertop, creating a "sink." (The word "sink" was borrowed from the landscape. It was a country term for a basin or low ground where water collected after a rain.) Finally, they enclosed the shelf under the sink to keep dirt and soot from settling in the buckets of water. The end result looked more like a cabinet than a bench.

The dry sink you see here is a traditional country form, though a fairly sophisticated design. The splashguards are incorporated in the front, back, and sides of the cabinet. (Usually, they were tacked on around the top, like an afterthought.) There is a drawer beneath the sink to store soap, washcloths, and so forth. (Some bucket benches had a small shelf just beneath the counter-top for these items.) In other words, this is a top-of-the-line, state-of-the-art dry sink, something you would expect to find in only the best country homes. ✺

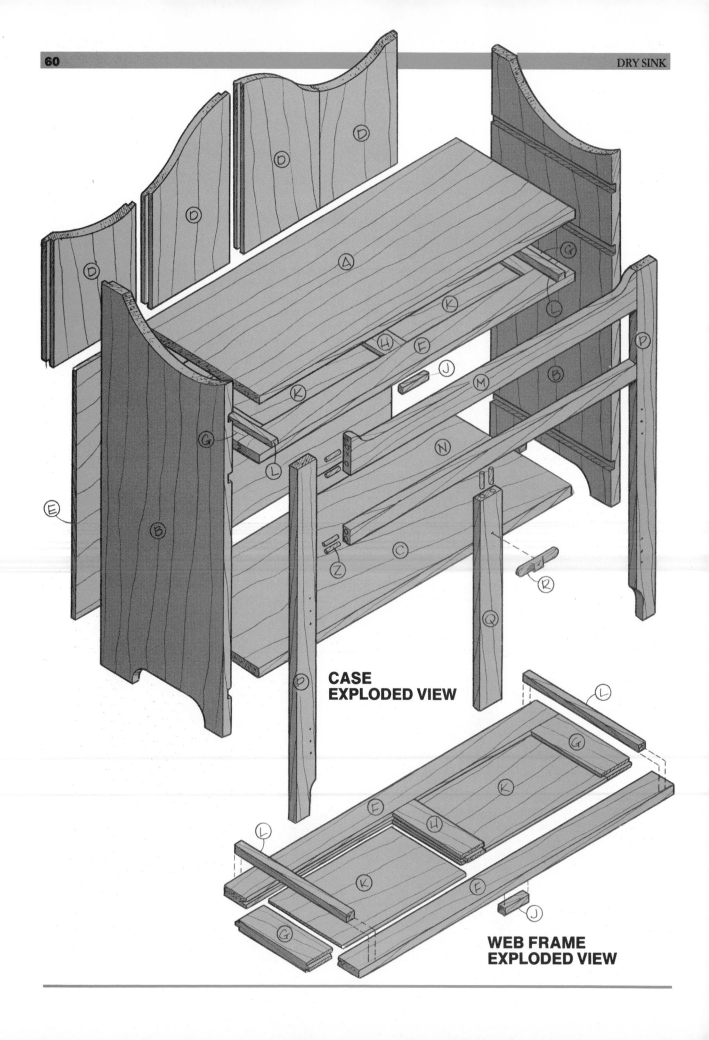

**CASE
EXPLODED VIEW**

**WEB FRAME
EXPLODED VIEW**

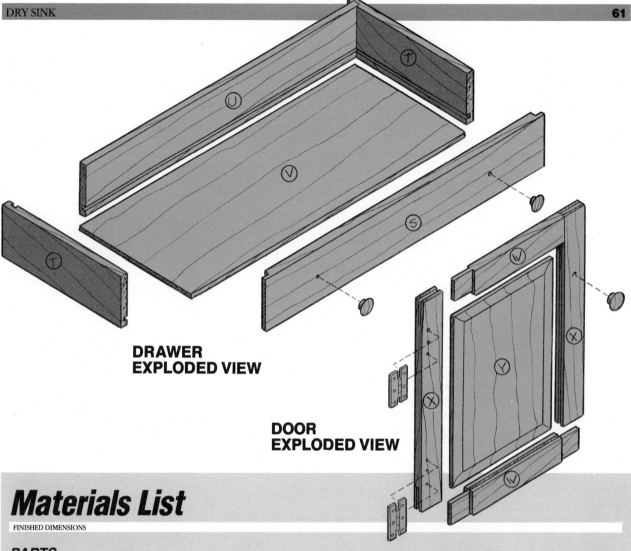

**DRAWER
EXPLODED VIEW**

**DOOR
EXPLODED VIEW**

Materials List

FINISHED DIMENSIONS

PARTS

A. Top shelf   ¾" x 13" x 35¼"

B. Sides (2)   ¾" x 13¾" x 36"

C. Bottom shelf   ¾" x 13⅜" x 35¼"

D. Back
splashguards (4)   ¾" x 9" x 16¼"

E. Back   ⅜" x 20⅞" x 35¼"

F. Web frame
rails (2)   ¾" x 2½" x 35¼"

G. Web frame end
stiles (2)   ¾" x 3" x 8¾"

H. Web frame
middle stile   ¾" x 2½" x 8¾"

J. Cleat   ¾" x ¾" x 2½"

K. Dust shields (2)   ¼" x 8¾" x 14⅛"

L. Drawer guides (2)   ¾" x ¾" x 13"

M. Front splashguard   ¾" x 3¾" x 31"

N. Face frame rail   ¾" x 1½" x 31"

P. Face frame
end stiles   ¾" x 2½" x 33¼"

Q. Face frame
middle stile   ¾" x 2½" x 19¾"

R. Latch   ½" x ¾" x 4"

S. Drawer front   ¾" x 4⅞" x 30⅞"

T. Drawer sides (2)   ¾" x 4⅞" x 13½"

U. Drawer back   ¾" x 4⅞" x 30⅛"

V. Drawer bottom   ¼" x 12½" x 30⅛"

W. Door rails (4)   ¾" x 2¼" x 14⅛"

X. Door stiles (4)   ¾" x 2¼" x 19¹¹/₁₆"

Y. Door panels (2) ¾" x 10⅛" x 15¹¹/₁₆"

Z. Face frame
dowels (10)   ⅜" dia. x 2"

HARDWARE

Door/drawer pulls (4)

2½" H-hinges and mounting screws
(2 pairs)

#12 x 1¼" Roundhead wood screw
and washer

#8 x 1¼" Flathead wood screws (24-30)

1" Brads (18-24)

⅝" Brads (6-8)

¾" Turn buttons (8)

1

Cut the parts to size. Carefully choose the wood to make this dry sink. Because this project has "flush" doors and a "flush" drawer, you need clear, kiln-dried *cabinet-grade* stock. Lesser grades of wood may warp or twist slightly. If this happens the doors and drawer will fit poorly.

To make this project, you'll need approximately 32 board feet of ¾"-thick lumber, a half sheet of ¼"-thick plywood, a quarter sheet of ⅜"-thick plywood, and three feet of ⅜"-diameter dowel. Glue up wide stock for the sides. When the glue dries thoroughly, cut the parts to the sizes shown in the Materials List.

2

Cut the joinery in the sides and back splashguards. The sides and back splashguards are joined to each other (and to other parts of the case) with dadoes and rabbets. Cut the rabbets first: Rout ¼"-wide, ⅜"-deep rabbets in the edges of the splashguards where they join each other, and ⅜"-wide, ⅜"-deep rabbets in the *outside* edges of the *outside* splashguards, as shown in *Back Splashguards, Top View.* Also, rout a ⅜" x ⅜" rabbet in the back edge of the sides.

Rout ¾"-wide, ⅜"-deep dadoes in the inside surface of the sides, where shown in the *Side Layout.* Use a straightedge clamped to the side, to guide your router. (See Figure 1.) Make each dado in several passes, cutting ⅛" deeper with each pass.

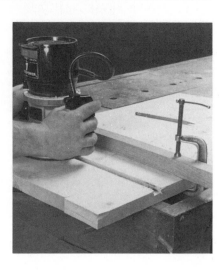

1/Clamp a straightedge to the sides to guide the router when you cut the dadoes. Make each dado in several passes, cutting ⅛" deeper with each pass.

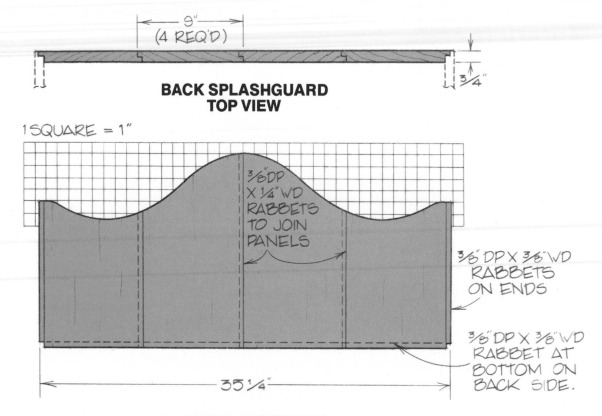

BACK SPLASHGUARD TOP VIEW

9"
(4 REQ'D)

¾"

1 SQUARE = 1"

⅜"DP X ¼"WD RABBETS TO JOIN PANELS

⅜" DP X ⅜"WD RABBETS ON ENDS

⅜"DP X ⅜"WD RABBET AT BOTTOM ON BACK SIDE.

35¼"

BACK SPLASHGUARD FRONT VIEW

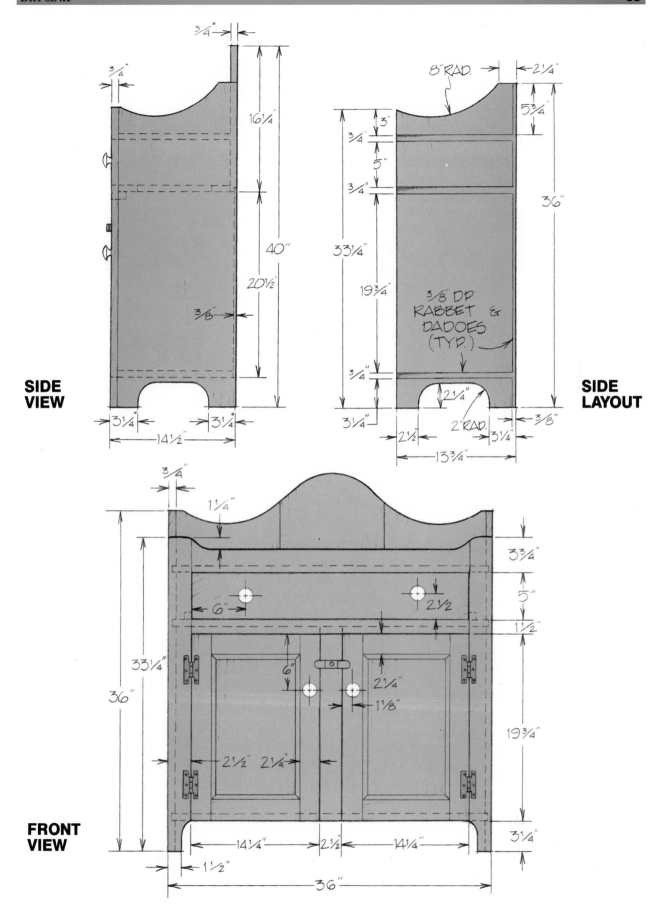

3/4"

3/4"

8" RAD.

2 1/4"

16 1/4"

5 3/4"

3"

3/4"

5"

3/4"

40"

33 1/4"

36"

20 1/2"

19 3/4"

3/8 DP RABBET & DADOES (TYP.)

3/8"

3/4"

2 1/4"

SIDE VIEW

SIDE LAYOUT

3 1/4"

3 1/4"

3 1/4"

2" RAD.

3/8"

14 1/2"

2 1/2"

13 3/4"

3/4"

1 1/4"

33 1/4"

5"

6"

2 1/2"

1 1/2"

33 1/4"

6"

2 1/4"

1 1/8"

36"

19 3/4"

2 1/2"

2 1/4"

FRONT VIEW

3 1/4"

14 1/4"

2 1/2"

14 1/4"

1 1/2"

36"

3

Make the web frame.   The drawer is supported by a "web frame," inside the dry sink case. Assemble this frame with tongue-and-groove joinery. With a dado cutter or a router, cut ¼" wide, ⅜"-deep grooves in all the *inside* edges of the rails and stiles. (See Figure 2.) Then cut ¼"-wide, ⅜"-long tenons or "tongues" in the ends of the stiles. (See Figure 3.) Glue the rails and stiles together with the dust shields in place. *Do not* glue the dust shields in the grooves. Let them "float," so that the assembly can expand and contract with changes in humidity.

When you clamp the web frame rails and stiles together, check that the assembly is square. The completed frame must be square if the drawer is to slide easily in and out of the case. After the glue dries on the rails and stiles, attach the drawer guides to the *top* surface of the web frame, and the cleat to the bottom surface, where shown in the *Web Frame, Top View.*

2/Cut a groove down the inside *edges of the web frame parts. If you use a table saw and dado cutter, guide the work with the rip fence.*

3/Cut the tongues in the ends of the web frame stiles with the same setup. Use the miter gauge to guide the work, and a stop block to gauge the length of the tongues.

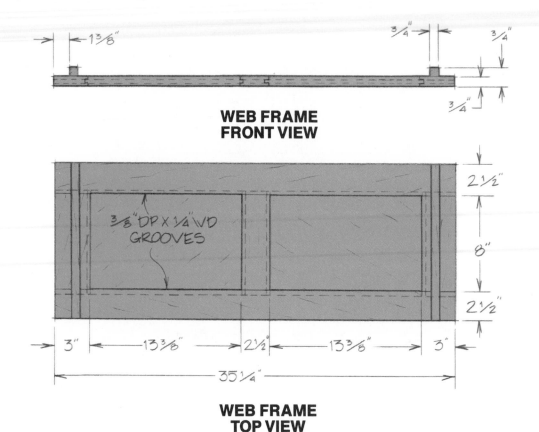

**WEB FRAME
FRONT VIEW**

**WEB FRAME
TOP VIEW**

4

Make the front frame. Dowel the members of the front frame together. Use a doweling jig as a guide for drilling the dowels holes in the frame members. Glue the end stile to the end rails. However, *do not* glue the middle stile in place yet; wait until you assemble the case — it will make the assembly easier. Once again, be sure that this frame is square when you clamp it up.

TRY THIS! If you have a "biscuit machine," you can join the face frame parts with biscuits. This saves a great deal of time over doweling.

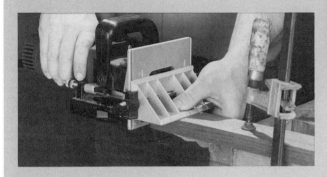

5

Cut the shapes of the sides and front splashguard. With a band saw or a sabre saw, cut the shapes of the sides and front splashguard as shown in the *Side Layout* and *Front Splashguard Pattern*. Sand the sawn edges to remove the saw marks. Do not cut the other shaped parts yet; wait until you assemble the case.

1 SQUARE = 1"

FRONT PATTERN

6

Assemble the dry sink case. Finish sand the sides, top and bottom shelves, back splashguards, and face frame (including the middle stile). Dry assemble the case to check the fit of the parts. When you're satisfied with the fit, reassemble the case with glue and screws. Counterbore and countersink the screws, then cover the heads with wooden plugs. Attach the back to the case with glue and brads.

TRY THIS! For an authentic "country" look, use square "cut" nails to attach the face frame to the case, instead of screws. Don't cover the heads of the nails; just let them show. Be careful when you drive these nails. You have to drill pilot holes; otherwise, the nails split the wood.

7

Cut the shapes of back splashguards and front end stiles. Using a sabre saw, cut the shapes of the back splashguards and the front end stiles, following the patterns shown in the *Front View* and the *Back Splashguard, Front View.* Sand the sawn edges to remove the saw marks.

8

Make the drawer. Cut the joinery in the drawer parts: The front is joined to the sides with ¾"-wide, ½"-deep rabbets, and the back with ¾"-wide, ⅜"-deep dadoes. The drawer bottom floats in a ¼"-wide, ⅜"-deep groove cut in the inside surface of the other parts. Make all of these joints with a router or a dado cutter.

Dry assemble the drawer to check the fit of the parts. If the fit is good, reassemble the front, back, and sides with glue. *Do not* glue the bottom in the grooves, just let it float. Reinforce the front-to-side rabbet joints with screws. Be sure that the drawer is square when you clamp it together; otherwise, it may not work properly.

Test the fit of the assembled drawer in the case. If it rubs or binds, plane and sand a little stock off the part that rubs. When the drawer slides easily in and out of the case, rub the bottom edges of the sides with wax. This will help the drawer work smoothly.

9

Make the doors. Using a tenon-cutting jig, make tenons in the ends of the door rails and "open" mortises in the ends of the door stiles. (See Figure 4.) Assemble the door frames with glue, and reinforce the corner joints with dowel pegs, as shown in the *Door Frame Joinery Detail.* Once again, the importance of making the assemblies square cannot be overemphasized.

When the glue dries on the door frames, rout the inside back of the frame, making a ⅜"-wide, ¼"-deep rabbet all around the inside edge. Square the corners of this rabbet with a chisel.

The door panels are "raised." To do this, "cove" cut the edges of the panels, running them across your table saw blade at 50° off square. Clamp a straightedge to the table saw to guide the work, and cut the coves in several passes, cutting just ⅛" deeper with each pass. (See Figure 5.) Stop when the coves are ½" deep.

Finish sand the door frames and door panels. Be sure to remove all the saw marks from the panels where you

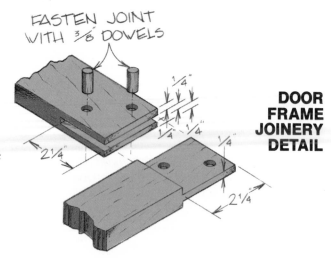

FASTEN JOINT WITH ⅜ DOWELS

DOOR FRAME JOINERY DETAIL

made the cove cuts. Mount the panels in the frame, keeping them in place with small metal turn buttons (also called "turn dogs" in some hardware stores). *Do not* glue the panels in place; just let them float in the rabbets.

4/Use a tenoning jig to cut both the mortises and the tenons that join the door frames. The jig you see here is store-bought, but you can easily make one from scraps of wood.

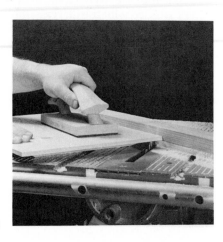

5/Pass the panels across the saw blade at 50° off square to make the cove cuts. Make these cuts in several passes, raising the blade just ⅛" higher with each pass.

10

Mount the doors in the case. Check the fit of the doors in the case. There should be a 1/16″ gap between the door frame and the face frame on all adjacent edges. If the door binds, use a block plane to remove a little stock from the parts of the frames that rub. When the doors fit to your satisfaction, mount them to the case with H-hinges.

TRY THIS! If you want the doors to fit perfectly, build them 1/16″-1/8″ oversize, then plane them down to fit the case.

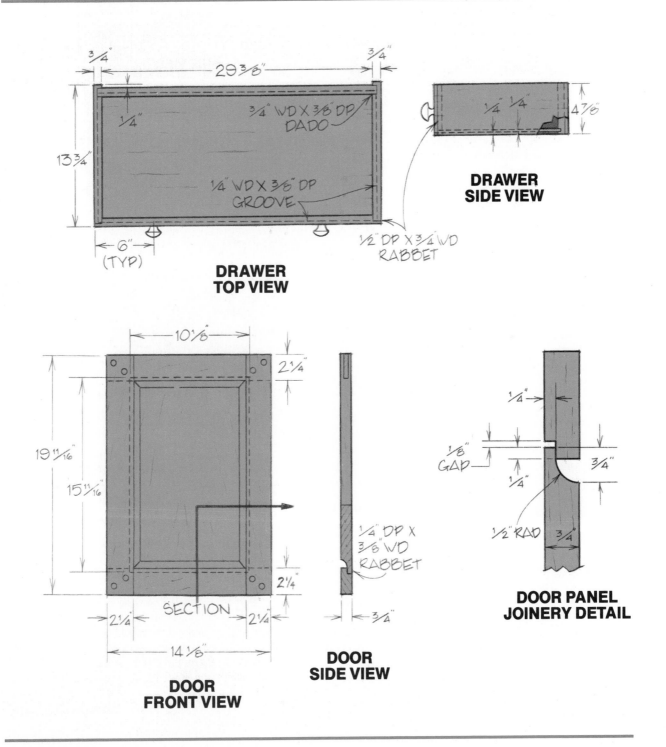

DRAWER SIDE VIEW

DRAWER TOP VIEW

DOOR FRONT VIEW

DOOR SIDE VIEW

DOOR PANEL JOINERY DETAIL

11

Make and install a door latch. Cut and shape the latch, according to the *Latch Details*. This latch is really a large, wooden turn button with two ends. When mounted on the middle stile, it keeps both doors closed. Sand the saw marks off the latch, then attach it to the case with a roundhead screw and washer. Don't tighten the screw too tight; just "snug it up" so that the latch turns easily — but not too easily.

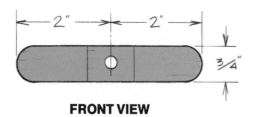

FRONT VIEW

SIDE VIEW

LATCH DETAILS

TRY THIS! The rustic wooden latch on the outside of the dry sink may not appeal to your taste. You may want something more "finished" in appearance. If this is the case, there are several options. You can install regular mechanical or magnetic cabinet door catches on the inside of the case, where they won't show. Or, if you want something more authentic, make a wooden "latch-and-pull" for each of the doors. The door pull turns a latch on the inside of the door, as shown in the drawing. When the door is closed, the latch rests against a wedge that is glued to the middle stile. This keeps the door closed snugly.

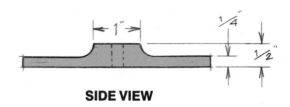

LATCH DETAIL
(SIDE VIEW)

WEDGE AND
LATCH ASSEMBLY

12

Finish the dry sink. Remove the drawer, doors, and latch from the case, and remove the panels from the doors. Do any touch-up sanding on parts that still need it, then apply a finish to the project. We gave our dry sink two coats of the traditional "milk paint." However, this project looks just as good in a variety of stains and finishes.

TRY THIS! Some of the better-equipped dry sinks were made with a copper- or tin-lined sink, to protect the wood. If you want, you can have a lining made up by almost any heating and air conditioning contractor that has his own sheet metal shop.

Milk Paint Finishes

One of the most popular country finishes was "milk paint." The lasting properties of this paint are legendary. In historical homes throughout New England and the Midwest, there are examples of milk paint finishes that are well over 200 years old, and they still look almost new.

The settlers mixed up their milk paint from materials they had on hand — spoiled milk, linseed oil, lime, and various natural pigments that they dug out of the earth or extracted from plants. For those of you who want to apply a milk paint finish to a country project today, there are several suppliers of "ready-mix" paint, made from dried milk products. Here are two sources:

> The Genuine Milk Paint Company
> P.O. Box 222
> Groton, MA 01450
>
> Country Way
> 206 Summit Place Drive
> Dunwoody, GA 30338

To use these commercial paints, simply mix the powder with the appropriate amount of water. Early milk paints (before the nineteenth century) were quite thick, so you might want to use less water to duplicate these finishes. Later on, the settlers used a thinner milk paint like a stain, so that the wood grain would show through the finish. To duplicate this effect, you, of course, use more water. (See Figures A and B.) In either case, mix thoroughly and strain the paint through cheesecloth to remove any lumps.

Before applying the paint, wet the raw wood with a damp cloth. Then spread a thin coat of paint with a sponge brush or some other cheap applicator. Keep mixing the paint as you work — the pigment has a tendency to settle to the bottom. Let the first coat dry overnight, then apply a second coat, if desired. Store the unused paint in a refrigerator.

When you have finished painting, rub the finish down with #00 steel wool. To make the finish look worn, rub a little harder at the edges and corners of the project, so that some of the lighter-colored wood begins to show. (See Figure C.) Seal the finish by wiping on a thin coat of boiled linseed oil. Rub the oiled finish with a clean cloth until you get a nice sheen.

A "fast" milk paint finish can be made from ordinary latex paint. Thin the paint 1:1 with water. Paint this thinned paint onto the surface of the project and, before it dries, wipe it down with a damp rag. Let the paint dry an hour or so; then apply a second coat, if you wish. When the finish dries completely, rub it down with steel wool and paste wax.

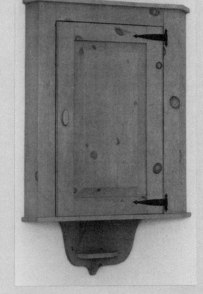

B/In the nineteenth century, country cabinetmakers began thinning the milk paint and applying it as a stain so that the wood grain would show slightly. On this piece the knots, in particular, are very visible.

C/To make the finish look old and worn, rub it with steel wool so that you remove a little extra paint from the corners and edges. These parts will appear lighter than the rest of the finish.

A/The grain of the wood does not show in this copy of an eighteenth century milk paint finish.

Country Village Cutting Boards

Silhouettes or "cut-outs" were a common form of country decoration. Visit a collection of folk art or "primitives" and you're likely to find the cut-out shapes of people, animals, buildings, vegetable and fruit — things familiar to country life.

These cut-out shapes had many uses. They adorned signs, weather-vanes, and mailboxes. Some were made into doorstops, key holders, and other useful objects; some simply filled the empty spaces on walls. Although the building cut-outs you see here will look good hung on your wall, as cutting boards they fall into the "useful" category. One side of each board is painted to look like a church, town hall, barn, or country house, and the other side is plain wood so that it can be used as a cutting board. There are four "feet" on the painted side of each board so that you can lay it down on a counter and not have to worry about scratching the paint.

There are several building cut-outs — a small country "village," if you use your imagination — for a good reason. Country cooks typically had several cutting boards so that the oils and juices from one type of food wouldn't contaminate another type. The four cutting boards you see here are meant to be used for meats, breads and pastries, fruits and "mild" vegetables (such as mushrooms and cucumbers), and "pungent" vegetables (such as onions and peppers).

Materials List

FINISHED DIMENSIONS

PARTS

A.	Church	7⁄8″ x 10″ x 12½″
B.	House	7⁄8″ x 9⅞″ x 12⅜″
C.	Barn	7⁄8″ x 11¼″ x 12¼″
D.	Town Hall	7⁄8″ x 11⅞″ x 12″
E.	Feet (16)*	½″ dia. x ½″

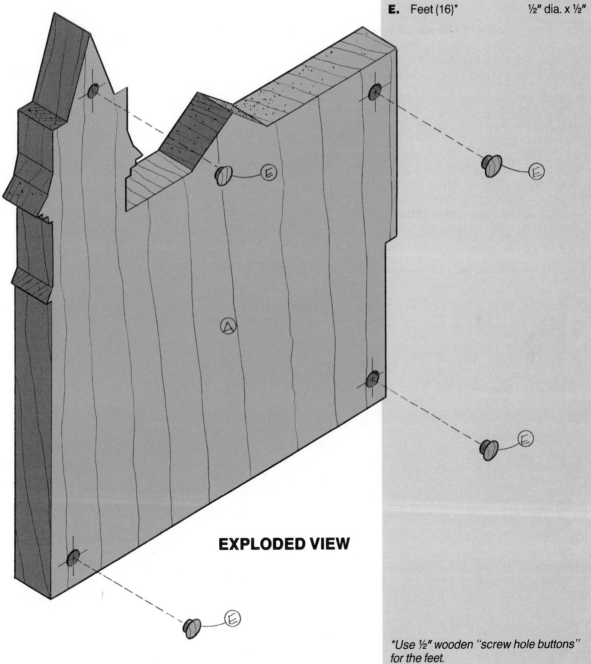

EXPLODED VIEW

Use ½″ wooden "screw hole buttons" for the feet.

1

Select the wood.   Because they will be in constant contact with moisture, cutting boards should be made from a dense, close-grained wood that absorbs water slowly. There are three domestic species that are particularly well-suited for this purpose — cherry, maple, and birch. Cherry develops a dark patina quickly, and this will affect the colors that you use to paint the features of the buildings, giving them an antique look. Maple and birch remain light for many years, and the colors will remain bright. Choose your wood for the effect you want to create.

2

Plane and cut the stock to size.
Purchase approximately 5 board feet of clear 4/4 ("four-quarters") hardwood, and plane it — or have it planed — to ⅞″ thick. The thicker the stock, the more resistant it will be to warping. If the stock is too thick, however, the cutting boards will be cumbersome. Cut them ⅛″-¼″ larger than the sizes shown in the Materials List.

TRY THIS!   To prevent the cutting boards from warping completely, rip the stock into 3″-wide strips; then glue it back together, edge to edge. Alternate the direction of the growth rings — one up, one down, and so on. Use a waterproof *epoxy* glue. Avoid resorcinol glue. Even though resorcinol is waterproof, it leaves dark lines at the glue joints. These may show through the paint.

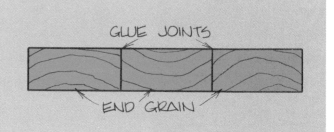

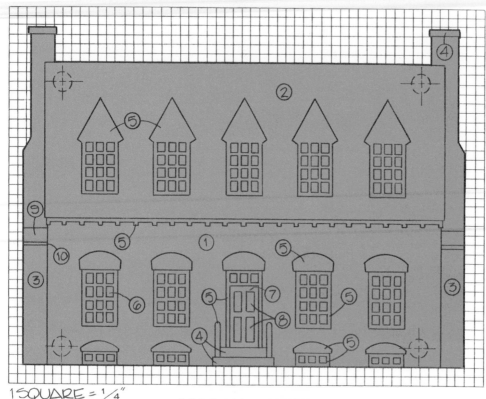

COLORS
1. WILLIAMSBURG BLUE
2. CHARCOAL BLACK
3. BRICK RED
4. LIGHT GREY
5. WHITE
6. MED. BLUE-GREY
7. RUST RED
8. RUST RED (DARKENED)
9. BRICK RED (LIGHTENED)
10. BRICK RED (DARKENED)

1 SQUARE = ¼″

COLONIAL HOUSE

3 ***Enlarge the patterns and affix them to the stock.*** Enlarge the patterns shown here, and make *two* photocopies of each full-size pattern. Use one copy as a cutting and drilling guide, and the second to transfer the features of the buildings to the cut-outs. (The first copy gets pretty beat up during the cutting and drilling processes.) Cover the backs of the first set of patterns with a spray adhesive and stick them to the stock. (See Figure 1.)

TRY THIS! If you live in a country house and you're particularly proud of it, draw a front view of it and substitute this for the house pattern. You might also want to use the town hall, a church, or other buildings from your own hometown.

*1/*You'll need to make two full size copies of each of the patterns. The first copy gets pretty beat up when you saw the shapes of the cutting boards.

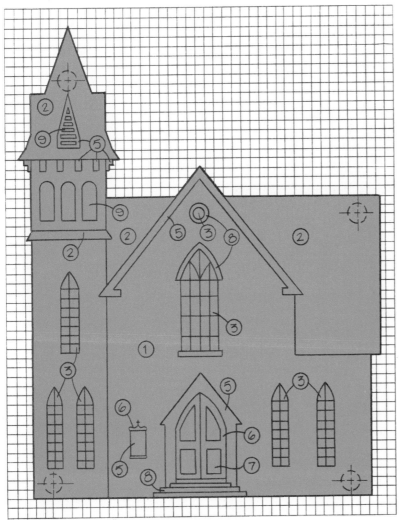

COLORS
1. SANDSTONE
2. SLATE BROWN
3. MED. BLUE-GREY
4. LIGHT GREY
5. WHITE
6. WALNUT BROWN
7. WALNUT BROWN (DARKENED)
8. CREAM
9. CHARCOAL

1 SQUARE = ¼"

CHURCH

4 **Cut the shapes of the buildings.** With a scroll saw, cut the shape of each building. Use a fine blade that leaves a smooth cut, and take it slow. Fine blades tend to overheat in hard, dense woods.

5 **Drill the holes for the feet.** In each cut-out, drill four stopped holes, ½″ in diameter and ¼″ deep. The positions of these holes are marked by *dotted* lines on each of the patterns.

6 **Finish sand the cut-outs.** Peel the patterns from the stock and wipe the wood down with acetone to remove any trace of the spray adhesive. Sand the saw marks from the edges of the cut-outs; then finish sand both faces to the glass-smooth surface.

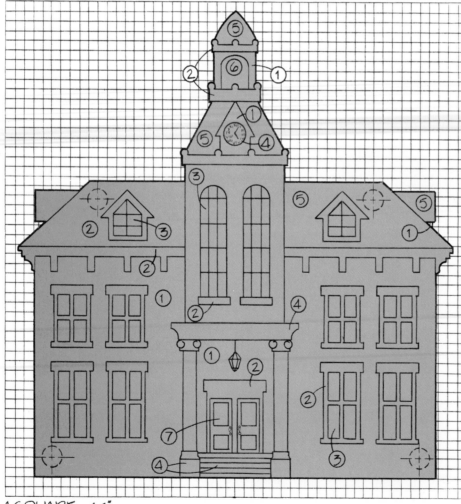

COLORS
1. MED. GREY
2. LIGHT GREY
3. MED. BLUE-GREY
4. WHITE
5. DARK GREY-BROWN
6. CHARCOAL
7. WALNUT BROWN

1 SQUARE = ¼″

COURTHOUSE

7 **Transfer the features of the buildings to the stock.** Tape carbon paper to one side of the cut-outs, carbon-face down. Over this, tape the second copy of the patterns. Trace the features of the buildings with a ball-point pen. The carbon paper will transfer the lines to the wood.

TRY THIS! If you don't have carbon paper handy, rub the backs of the patterns with a #2 lead pencil. Tape the patterns to the stock and trace the features with a pen. The pencil will deposit enough graphite on the paper patterns to transfer the lines without the use of carbon paper.

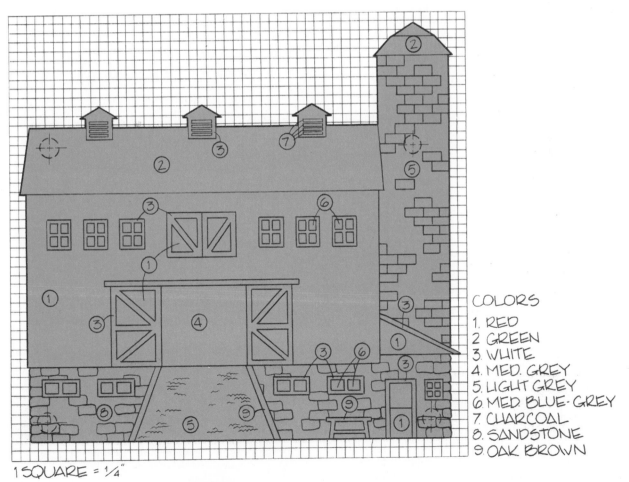

COLORS

1. RED
2. GREEN
3. WHITE
4. MED. GREY
5. LIGHT GREY
6. MED. BLUE-GREY
7. CHARCOAL
8. SANDSTONE
9. OAK BROWN

1 SQUARE = ¼"

BARN

8 Burn or carve the features into the stock.

The features should be made a permanent part of the cut-outs. There are two relatively simple techniques you can use to do this. The first is to trace the lines with a woodburning tool. The second is to trace them with a "groover" or V-shaped carving chisel. (See Figure 2.) Apply a dark stain to the wood; then sand it off, leaving the stain in the grooves only. Whatever method you use, take care that the lines are an even width and depth. Practice on a piece of scrap stock before you burn or carve the cut-outs.

2/You must somehow outline the details of the pattern, so that they stand out. This can be done with a woodburning tool, as shown here, or by cutting a V-groove with a chisel.

9 Glue the feet in place.

Using waterproof epoxy, glue the feet in the stopped holes in the cut-outs. You can use ordinary ½"-diameter dowels for these feet, although screw hole buttons work and look so much better. These "buttons" are available in some building supply centers and through most mail-order woodworking supply houses.

10 Paint the features of the buildings.

Once you've made the lines, color in between them. Paint the edges, too. The patterns are color-coded to help you decide what color to put where. However, these are just suggestions. You can make up your own color scheme.

There are many, many types of paints and dyes that you can use to color the building cut-outs, and you probably have your own preferences. We experimented with two — artists oils and acrylics — and found these produced two different effects. We thinned the oils with linseed oil and applied them like a stain, so that you could see the wood grain underneath the color. We also tried thinning the acrylics (with water), but they became splotchy. In order for the colors to remain even, we had to apply the acrylics fairly thick. You couldn't see the wood grain under them.

Whatever paints or dyes you decide to use, experiment with them on a piece of scrap *before* you start coloring the cut-outs. Try several different colors. Different colors may require modestly different application techniques, even though they're the same type of paint. For example, when experimenting with acrylics, we found that the red was much harder to apply evenly than the other colors. We had to paint that color on very thick, almost straight from the tube. You may find similar differences among the colors that you choose.

11 Finish the cutting boards.

After the paint has dried completely, lightly rub it with #0000 steel wool. Sand off any paint that may have gotten on the "cutting" side of the cutting boards. Apply several coats of "salad-bowl dressing" to all surfaces of the boards. This non-toxic finish is available at some paint stores and through most woodworking supply houses.

TRY THIS! If you want the cut-outs to have a used, antique look, rub them with #0 steel wool. Rub hard enough that the wood begins to show through the paint in places.

12 *Make the display shelves (optional).*

If you don't have a place to display your finished cutting boards, you may want to make the simple, narrow "bracket" shelves shown here. Make two — each shelf holds two cutting boards.

Cut the parts to size, and cut the lip in the front of the shelves on your table saw. (Notice that the top surface of the shelf behind the lip is angled slightly. This is done so that the cutting boards will tilt back against the wall when you rest them on the shelves.) Use a band saw or scroll saw to cut the shapes of the bracket and valance. Sand the parts, and assemble them with glue and screws. Counterbore and countersink the screws, then hide the

screw heads with wooden plugs. If you wish, apply a grass-and-dandelions stencil to the front edge of the shelves. Then stain and finish the shelves to suit yourself.

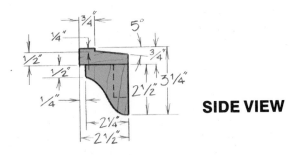

SIDE VIEW

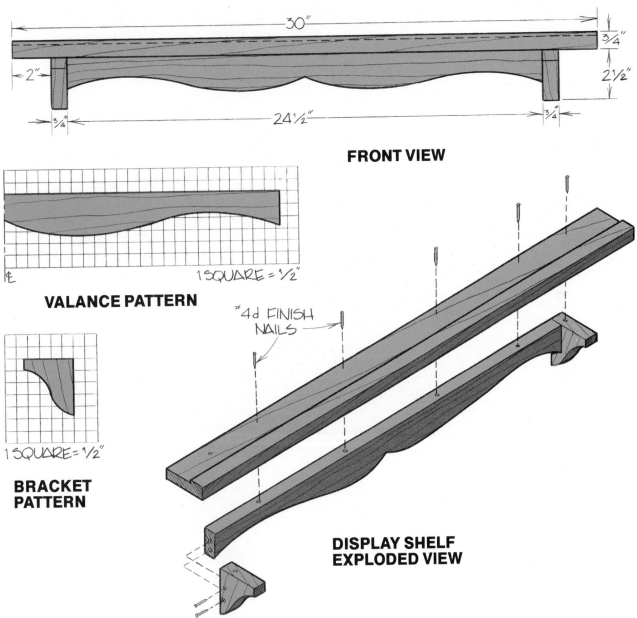

FRONT VIEW

VALANCE PATTERN

1 SQUARE = ½"

BRACKET PATTERN

1 SQUARE = ½"

#4d FINISH NAILS

DISPLAY SHELF EXPLODED VIEW

Spice Chest

Spices and herbs were a precious commodity to the settlers. They didn't have the variety of foods that we have today, and without a store of spices, their meals would have been bland and monotonous. They didn't have over-the-counter medicines, either. Instead, they collected and stored many different herbs to treat a wide assortment of ailments. Clearly, the "spice chest" was an important fixture in the country kitchen. This was a spice rack, first aid center, and medicine cabinet all rolled into one.

Today, a spice chest still makes an excellent place to store and organize spices. Or it can hold hand towels, dish cloths, napkins, and other small linens that you use in the kitchen and dining room. By substituting glass for the wood panel in the door, you can also use it to display small collectibles.

We've designed the country spice chest to store or display almost any small item that you may have. The inside shelves are adjustable, so that you can raise or lower them as your needs dictate. The wooden door panel can be easily replaced by a pane of glass, so that you can see the contents of the chest. And there's a "salt box" bin underneath the case to collect keys, change, matches, and similar pocket-sized things.

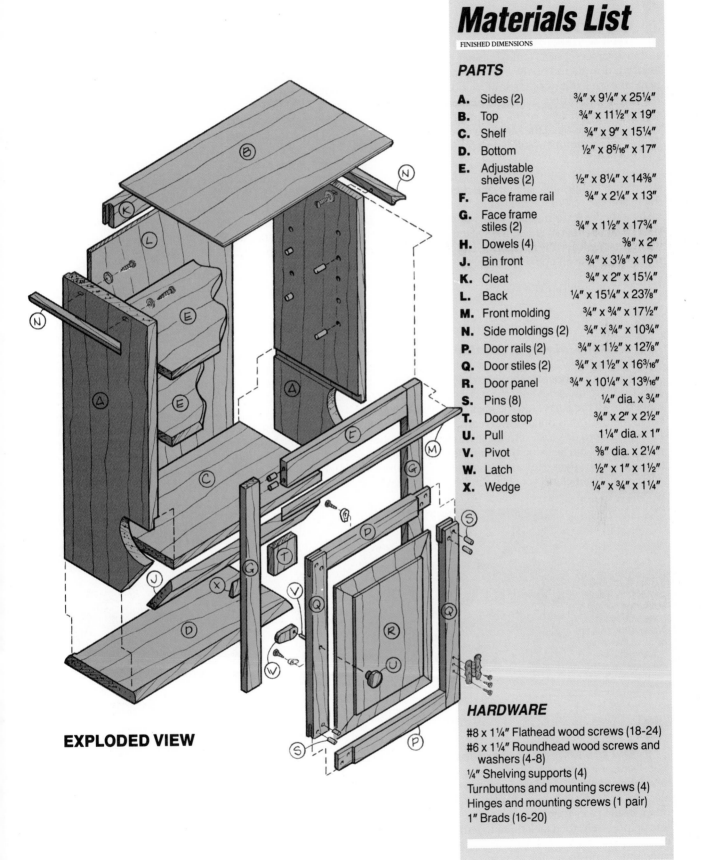

EXPLODED VIEW

Materials List

FINISHED DIMENSIONS

PARTS

A.	Sides (2)	¾" x 9¼" x 25¼"
B.	Top	¾" x 11½" x 19"
C.	Shelf	¾" x 9" x 15¼"
D.	Bottom	½" x 8⁵⁄₁₆" x 17"
E.	Adjustable shelves (2)	½" x 8¼" x 14⅜"
F.	Face frame rail	¾" x 2¼" x 13"
G.	Face frame stiles (2)	¾" x 1½" x 17¾"
H.	Dowels (4)	⅜" x 2"
J.	Bin front	¾" x 3⅛" x 16"
K.	Cleat	¾" x 2" x 15¼"
L.	Back	¼" x 15¼" x 23⅞"
M.	Front molding	¾" x ¾" x 17½"
N.	Side moldings (2)	¾" x ¾" x 10¾"
P.	Door rails (2)	¾" x 1½" x 12⅞"
Q.	Door stiles (2)	¾" x 1½" x 16³⁄₁₆"
R.	Door panel	¾" x 10¼" x 13⁹⁄₁₆"
S.	Pins (8)	¼" dia. x ¾"
T.	Door stop	¾" x 2" x 2½"
U.	Pull	1¼" dia. x 1"
V.	Pivot	⅜" dia. x 2¼"
W.	Latch	½" x 1" x 1½"
X.	Wedge	¼" x ¾" x 1¼"

HARDWARE

#8 x 1¼" Flathead wood screws (18-24)
#6 x 1¼" Roundhead wood screws and washers (4-8)
¼" Shelving supports (4)
Turnbuttons and mounting screws (4)
Hinges and mounting screws (1 pair)
1" Brads (16-20)

1

Cut the parts to size. To build this project, you'll need approximately 16 board feet of 4/4 ("four-quarters") or 1"-thick cabinet grade lumber, plus assorted dowels and hardware. You may, if you choose, make the back out of either solid wood or ¼" plywood. If you select plywood, the face veneer should match or complement the solid wood, since you'll see the back whenever you look in the bin. A plywood back will also decrease the amount of solid lumber you'll need by about 2 board feet.

Once you have gathered your materials, plane the stock for the adjustable shelves and the bottom to ½" thick, and the rest of the lumber to ¾" thick. If you're making the back from solid wood, resaw the lumber on your band saw to ⁵⁄₁₆" thick, then plane it to ¼". If you wish, you can leave the back surface of the back stock rough, since it won't be seen.

Cut the parts to the sizes shown in the Materials List, except for the moldings. Set this stock aside for the moment.

■ When you cut the bin front, bevel-rip the bottom edge at 15°.

■ You may wish to cut the door parts about ⅛" longer and wider than given. When you build the door, it will be too large to fit the opening, and you can plane down the edges to get a perfect fit.

■ If you make the back from solid wood, cut it into strips 25⅞" long and 2" or 3" wide. Later on, when you assemble the back to the case, this arrangement will let the back expand and contract with changes in temperature and humidity without splitting or distorting the case.

■ Don't cut the sides to shape now. There's work to be done on them first.

2

Cut the joinery in the sides, bottom, and cleat. With a router or a dado cutter, make the dadoes and the rabbets in the sides, bottom, and cleat. The dadoes in the sides hold the fixed shelf, while the rabbets in all the parts hold the back. Note that the rabbet in the bottom is blind at both ends, as shown in the *Bottom Layout*. It's easiest to make this sort of a rabbet with a router, and just stop the tool before the bit cuts through to the edges. However, don't square the blind edges of the rabbet just yet. Wait until you fit the bottom to the case.

Drill ¼"-diameter, ½"-deep stopped holes in the inside faces of the sides, as shown in the *Side Layout*. These holes will hold the shelving supports for the adjustable shelves.

Drill *slotted* pilot holes near the top edge of the sides. You'll use these to attach the side moldings. Since the grain of the moldings is perpendicular to the grain of the sides, the slots allow the sides to expand and contract under the moldings. (See Figures 1 and 2.)

1/To drill a slotted pilot hole for a wood screw, first drill two holes side by side. These holes should be just a little larger than the shank of the screw.

2/Then angle the drill from side to side, working back and forth to remove the waste between the two holes.

3

Cut the shapes of the sides. With a band saw or a sabre saw, cut the shapes of the sides. Since these sides are identical, you can cut them exactly alike if you "pad saw" them. Stack them one on top of the other, inside faces touching. Make sure that the dadoes line up precisely, then tack them together with brads to make a "pad." Mark the shape and cut them both at the same time. Sand away the saw marks.

SIDE PATTERN

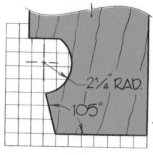

2¼" RAD.

105°

1 SQUARE = 1"

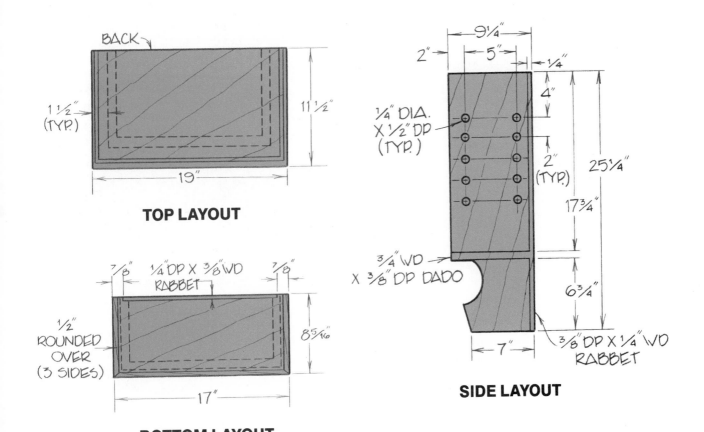

TOP LAYOUT

BOTTOM LAYOUT

SIDE LAYOUT

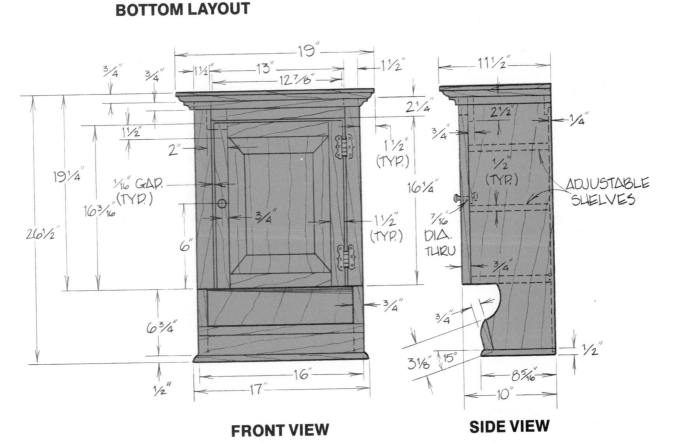

FRONT VIEW

SIDE VIEW

4 **Join the parts of the face frame.** Using a doweling jig to guide your drill, bore dowel holes to join the face frame rails and stile. "Dry" assemble the parts with dowels, but do not glue them together yet.

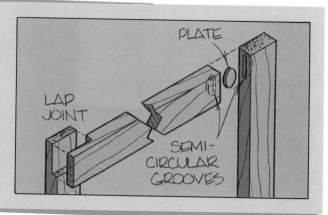

TRY THIS! There are several alternatives for joining face frame members. Among them: (1) You can use lap joints. You'll be able to see the end grain of the rails on the outside edge, but this was a common practice among many country cabinetmakers. (2) You can also join the parts with plates or "biscuits." This, however, requires a plate joining tool.

5 **Shape the edges of the top and bottom.** With a router or a shaper, machine the front and side edges of the top and the bottom of the case. The bottom is rounded with a ½" quarter-round bit, as shown in the *Bottom Edge Detail*, while the top gets the same treatment with a step, as shown in the *Top Molding Detail*. Sand away any millmarks left by the cutters.

BOTTOM EDGE DETAIL

TOP MOLDING DETAIL

6 **Make the molding stock.** While you're set up for shaping, make the cove molding stock for the top and side moldings. This process is very much like edge-shaping. Using a ½" cove bit, cut the shape of the molding into the edge of a wide board, then rip the shaped edge from the stock on a table saw. (See Figure 3.) Don't cut the moldings to length yet; wait until you've partially assembled the case.

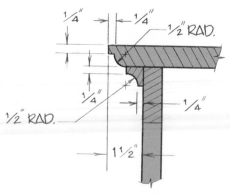

3/To make your own molding, rout the edge of a wide board, then rip the shaped edge from the stock. Don't try to make molding the other way around — ripping first, then routing. The narrow stock may come apart when you rout it.

7 **Finish sand all parts.** Finish sand all the parts and assemblies that you've made so far, including the molding stock. Be careful not to round or "break" any edges or faces where two parts will be joined.

8 Assemble the case, except for the top, bottom, and back.

Dry-assemble the parts of the case and the face frame to test their fit. Make any minor adjustments in the size and the shape of the parts that are necessary to get a good fit, then disassemble the case.

Assemble the face frame, gluing the parts together. While the glue cures on the frame, assemble the other parts of the case with glue, brads, and screws. First glue the bin front, shelf, and cleat to the sides. Hold the cleat in place with brads; the bin front and the shelf need no reinforcement. Finally, glue the face frame to the sides. *Do not* attach the top, bottom, or back at this time.

TRY THIS! If you wish to reinforce the glue joints holding the face frame and the bin front to the sides, use splines or some other *hidden* joinery. (We used "biscuits.") Avoid screws. Even if you cover the heads, the plugs will mar the appearance of the front of the case. In a few more steps, you'll use screws to fasten the top and bottom in place, then cover the heads with plugs. These plugs, however, are less visible, since this chest will most probably be hung at eye level. But you'll always be looking straight at the face frame, no matter how you place the completed project.

9 Attach the moldings to the case.

Carefully fit the molding to the case, joining the ends of the three pieces with miter joints. Glue the front molding in place, then attach the side moldings with glue and screws. (See Figure 4.)

Apply glue *only* to the mitered ends of the side moldings and perhaps the first 1″ of the adjoining face nearest the front of the case. *Do not* glue the remaining length of the moldings. As previously noted, the grain of these moldings opposes the grain of the sides. A long glue joint between these two parts will eventually give way. Instead, drive screws into the moldings through the slotted holes in the case. This will secure the side moldings to the case, but still allow the sides to expand and contract without stressing any other part of the assembly.

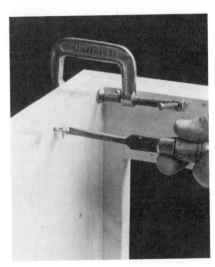

4/Screw (don't glue) the side moldings to the case. The top edge of the moldings must be flush with the top edge of the sides.

10 Attach the top and bottom to the case.

Screw the top and bottom to the assembly, counterboring and countersinking the screws.

Cover the screw heads with wooden plugs, and sand the plugs flush with the surface of the stock.

TRY THIS! If you want to avoid using screws and screw plugs altogether, attach the top and bottom with sliding (or "French") dovetail joints. This requires a good deal of precision, but the joinery is completely invisible from the front and sides when you complete the case.

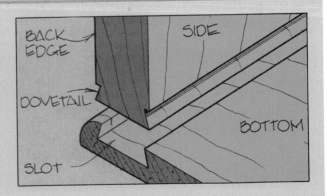

11

Assemble the door frame. With a table saw, cut the bridle joints (sometimes called slot or "open" mortises and tenons) that join the parts of the door frame. Because they are extremely strong, these joints are often used to join rails and stiles of assemblies that will see a lot of use — such as doors. For complete instructions on how to cut bridle joints, refer to *Step-by-Step: Making Bridle Joints.*

Assemble the door frame with glue. As you clamp up the rails and the stiles, check that the frame is square. After the glue cures, drill ¼"-diameter holes through the corners of the frame, as shown in the *Bridle Joint Detail.* Glue ¼"-diameter dowels in these holes, and sand them flush with the inside and outside face of the frame.

Note: These dowels are more decorative than functional. Their original purpose was to pin the bridle joints together and prevent the door frame from sagging, should the glue give way. However, with today's improved glues, there is little chance that this will happen if the joints are fitted properly.

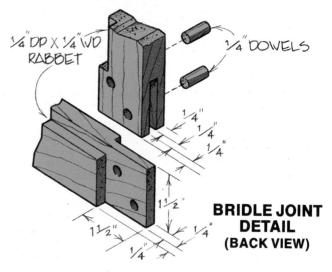

**BRIDLE JOINT
DETAIL
(BACK VIEW)**

Using either a straight bit or a rabbeting bit in your router, cut a ¼"-wide, ¼"-deep rabbet all around the inside edge of the door frame, on the inside face. With a hand chisel, square the corners of the rabbet. This rabbet will hold the door panel.

12

Cut the raised door panel. Attach a "tall" fence extension to your table saw rip fence. This is nothing more than a perfectly flat board, about 8" wide and as long as the fence. It will help you keep the panel stock at the proper angle to the blade as you cut the edge.

Tilt the blade (or the table) to 15°. Adjust the height of the blade and the position of the rip fence, then make a few test cuts in scrap stock. You want the blade to slice through the edge of the panel at an angle, leaving a ⅛" step on the front face, as shown in the *Door Frame and Panel Section.* When you have the fence and the blade adjusted properly, cut all four edges of the door panel. (See Figure 5.)

Test fit the door panel to the door frame. It should rest in the rabbet with about ¹⁄₁₆" of "slop" all the way around. The back face of the panel should be flush with or slightly recessed below the inside face of the frame. If the panel is too tight, sand or plane a little stock from the edges. If it sits too high in the rabbet, you have two choices: Cut the rabbet a little deeper, or re-make the panel.

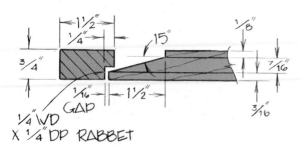

**DOOR FRAME
AND PANEL SECTION**

5/Use a hollow-ground planer blade to cut the raised door panel. This leaves a smooth cut that requires very little sanding.

13

Fit the door to the case. Glue the door stop to the inside surface of the upper part of the face frame, where shown on the *Front View*. The position of this stop is not critical, but you want it to back up the upper end of the same stile where you will install the pull and the latch. If you wish, reinforce the glue joint with a countersunk flathead wood screw. Drive this screw from *inside* the case.

When the glue on the stop cures, position the door frame inside the face frame. There should be a 1/16″ gap (approximately) between the two frames, all around the door. If necessary, plane or sand a little stock from the door frame to get a good fit. If you use a block plane, be certain that it's very sharp. Always push the plane in from the corners toward the middle of the stile or rail, to avoid chipping the frame.

14

Attach the pull and latch to the door frame. Purchase a 1¼″-diameter, unfinished wooden pull or turn your own on a lathe. In the back of the pull, where you would normally drill a pilot hole for a screw, drill a ⅜″-diameter, ¾-deep stopped hole. Glue the pivot — a ⅜″-diameter dowel — in this hole, and set the assembly aside for the glue to cure.

Drill a ⅜″-diameter hole through the latch where shown in the *Latch Detail*. Round the ends of the latch and cut a slight taper on one face. It's easy to do both the rounding and the tapering on a stationary belt or disc sander; however, you can also use a rasp, file, and sandpaper. In the door frame, drill a 7/16″-diameter hole through a stile, where shown in the *Front View* and *Side View*. This hole can be placed in either the right or the left stile, depending on which direction you want the door to open.

Insert the pivot through the hole in the stile from the outside, and glue the latch to the pivot on the inside of the door frame, as shown in the *Wedge and Latch Assembly*. *Do not* press the latch too far onto the pivot; you don't want the pull or the latch to be snug against the door frame. Instead, leave about 1/16″ of "slop" so that you can turn the latch easily by twisting the pull.

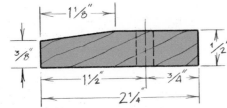

LATCH DETAIL (SIDE VIEW)

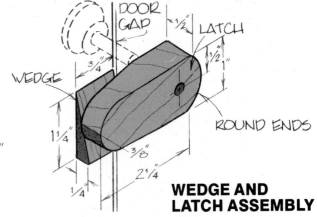

WEDGE AND LATCH ASSEMBLY

15

Assemble the door and hinge it to the case. Place the door panel in the door frame, so that it rests in the rabbets. Secure the panel to the frame with small "turnbuttons." (See Figure 6.) Then put the assembled door in place in the case and attach it to the face frame with hinges. (As shown, these are decorative hinges that sit on the outside surface of the face frame and door frame. However, you may also mortise ordinary butt hinges into the edges of the frames.)

With the door closed, reach into the case through the back and place the wedge under the latch, against the inside of the door frame. This wedge should be positioned so that when the latch is horizontal, the door will be held tight against the door stop and the shelf. Mark the position of the wedge, then glue it to the face frame.

6/Use turnbuttons to secure the panel in the door. You can find these in most hardware stores in the section where they keep screen door hardware.

16

Fit the back to the case. Square the blind ends of the rabbet in the back edge of the bottom. Fit the back (or back slats) into the rabbets in the back of the case. If you're making the back from solid wood, and have ripped the back stock into 2"-3" wide slats, place the slats so that there's a ¹⁄₃₂" gap (approximately) between them, to allow them to expand and contract. *Do not* attach the back to the case permanently at this time, just make sure of the fit.

17

Finish the completed spice chest. Remove the back and door from the case, and disassemble all the hardware. Finish sand any parts that may still need it, then apply a finish to the case.

It was customary to paint the inside of these spice chests white. This served two purposes: It made it easier to keep the inside clean, and it helped to lighten the interior so that small items could be easily found. If you want to follow this tradition when finishing your chest, mask off the bottom part of the back that will be visible (as the back of the bin) when you attach it to the case. Paint the top part white, and finish the bottom part as you have the rest of the case.

Step-by-Step: Making Bridle Joints

Bridle joints, or open mortise-and-tenon joints, are often used to join frame parts. Although these joints are extremely strong, they are the easiest mortises and tenons you can make.

To make them, however, you need a *tenoning jig*. Several tool manufacturers sell these jigs as accessories for their table saws. You can also make one from scraps of hardwood. The shop-made jig shown here rides along the rip fence.

Note: The quick-release clamp shown in the drawing can be purchased from several mail-order woodworking supply businesses. You may also be able to have your local hardware store special-order it for you.

Make the mortises in the stiles first. Clamp the stiles end down in the tenoning jig. Adjust the position of the rip fence so that it will guide the stock over the blade, cutting a ⅛"-wide kerf in the ends (half the width of the finished slots). Adjust the height of the blade so that the kerf will be as deep as the frame members are wide. Then cut the first half of the slot.

Turn the stock around and cut the other cheek. Repeat until you have cut all the cheeks of all the tenons.

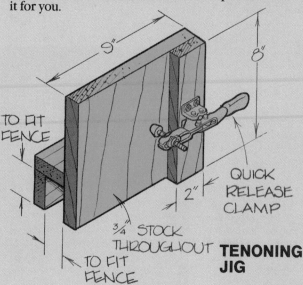

9"

8"

TO FIT FENCE

QUICK RELEASE CLAMP

2"

¾" STOCK THROUGHOUT

TO FIT FENCE

TENONING JIG

18

Assemble and hang the finished chest. Attach the back to the chest with brads, then reassemble the door and hinge it to the case. To hang the chest, drive screws through the cleat and into the wall studs. If you can't attach the chest directly to a stud, use molly anchors to attach it to the hollow parts of the wall.

Important note: While the spice chest isn't extremely heavy, it's got enough weight that you should attach it to at least one stud. Because of the width of the project, you'll probably have to use a combination of screws and mollies to hang it. Or: Don't hang the chest at all; simply set it on a countertop or table.

TRY THIS! Contemporary wall cabinets are often hung with the aid of "scarf" joints. The beveled edge of a cleat that has been attached to the wall mates with the beveled edge of another cleat that is attached to the cabinet. This arrangement makes it extremely easy to hang and remove a cabinet.

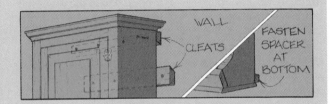

Turn the stock around and cut the second half of the slot. The slot mortise should now be ¼" wide. Repeat this procedure until you have cut all the mortises.

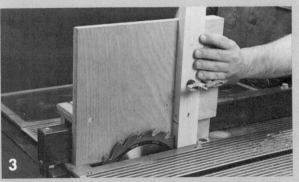

Readjust the position of the rip fence to cut the sides or "cheeks" of the tenons in the rails. Leave the blade height just as it is. Clamp the rails in the jig, and cut the first cheek of the tenons.

You won't need the jig to cut the shoulders of the tenons. Instead, use the stop block clamped to the rip fence to gauge the length of the tenons. Adjust the height of the blade to cut just the shoulders — you don't want to score the cheeks and perhaps weaken the tenons. Use the miter gauge to guide the stock over the blade. Cut the first shoulder…

…then turn the stock over and cut the second shoulder. Repeat until you have cut the shoulders of all the tenons.

Window Shelf

S pace was at a premium in most country homes. A typical log cabin might be smaller than a contemporary living room, and it would house an entire family. Consequently, country folk "made space" wherever they could.

This window shelf is one example of the way they did it. The shelf is actually a long, decorative "valance box" that mounts above the window and provides a place to hang curtains. While many such boxes are open at the top, this is not. Instead, it's topped with a narrow shelf that can be used to store spices, canned goods, dishes, or knickknacks.

As we designed the window shelf you see here, it has a ¾″-diameter wooden curtain rod that rests in two brackets, so that the curtains can be easily hung or removed. However, the rod and the brackets are optional. If you wish, you can substitute another type of rod, or eliminate the rod altogether and use the window shelf without curtains.

Materials List

FINISHED DIMENSIONS

PARTS

A.	Top	¾" x 5½" x (Variable)
B.	Front	¾" x 3¼" x (Variable)
C.	Sides (2)	¾" x 3¾" x 6"
D.	Cleat	¾" x 2" x (Variable)
E.	Hangers (2)	¾" x 1¾" x 2"
F.	Rod	¾" dia. x (Variable)

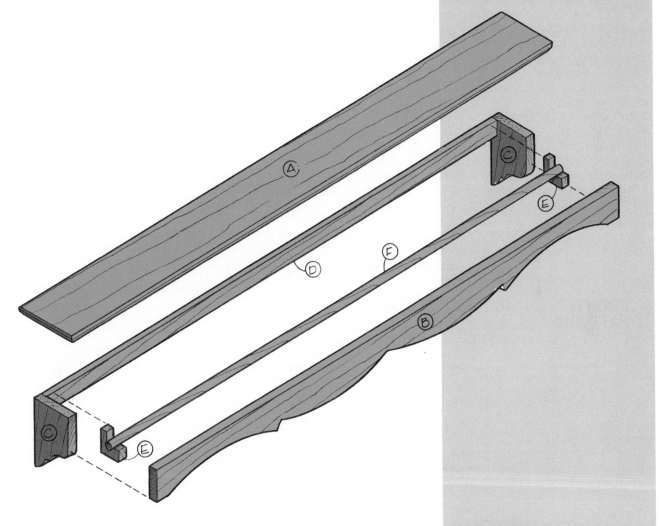

EXPLODED VIEW

HARDWARE

#10 x 1¼" Flathead wood screws (10-12)
#12 x 1¾" Flathead wood screws (2-4),
   or
³/₁₆" Molly anchors (2-4), or
¼"-dia. x 2½" Lag screws and lead
   expansion shields

1

Cut the parts to size.   First measure the width of your window (or the length of the sash, if you prefer to say it that way). Use this measurement to figure the length of the parts marked "variable" in the Materials List:

Length of top = Width of window + 6″
Length of front = Width of window + 3″
Length of cleat = Width of window + 1½″
Length of rod = Width of window + 1⅜″

Once you've figured the dimensions of all the parts, cut the stock to the sizes you need.

2

Cut the shapes of the sides and front.   Enlarge the *Side Pattern* and the *Front Pattern*. Remember, you will have to adjust the length of the front pattern to fit your stock. As shown, the pattern will fit a front 48″ long. For any other size, divide the length of the front you want by 48. This will give you the *horizontal* dimension of the squares on the pattern to use when you enlarge the pattern.

For example, if the length of the front of your window shelf is 36″, divide 36 by 48. The result is ¾. When you draw up the grid to enlarge the *Front Pattern,* make the squares 1″ high, but only ¾″ wide. Then sketch the shape of the pattern on the grid as you normally would.

When you have enlarged both patterns, trace these onto their respective boards. With a band saw or a sabre saw, cut the outside shapes of the sides and aprons. Sand off the saw marks from the cut edges.

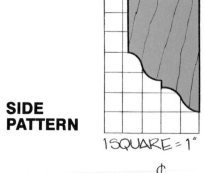

SIDE PATTERN

1 SQUARE = 1″

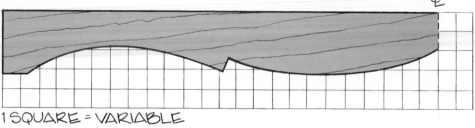

FRONT PATTERN

1 SQUARE = VARIABLE

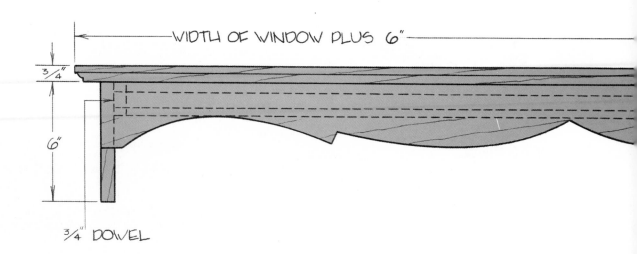

WIDTH OF WINDOW PLUS 6″

¾″

6″

¾″ DOWEL

FRONT VIEW

3 *Rout the shape of the top edge.* Using a
hand-held router, shape the sides and front edges
of the top. You can use the ogee shape we show in the
Front Edge Detail, or rout some other shape that you
prefer. Before you rout, make sure that the stock is
clamped firmly to your workbench. **Note:** You can also
use a shaper for this step, if you have one.

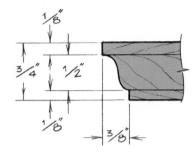

**FRONT EDGE
DETAIL**

4 *Make the hangers.* The hangers are open
at the top, so that you can easily put the rod in
place and remove it again. To make these hangers, drill
a $^{13}/_{16}$″-diameter hole through the hanger stock, where
shown in the *Hanger Layout.* Then "open up" this hole
by cutting in from the top and front edges, using a band
saw or coping saw.

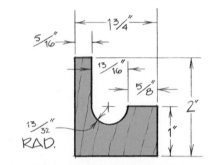

**HANGER
LAYOUT**

TRY THIS! To save yourself a little work,
"pad drill" and "pad saw" the hangers. Stack the
pieces and nail them together with 3d (1¼″-long)
finishing nails or brads to make a "pad." (If you're
making more than one window shelf, this pad can
be as tall as four ¾″-thick pieces.) The brads
should be placed in the waste part of the cleats,
but *not* where you will drill the hole. Mark the location of the hole and the cuts to open up the hole on
the top piece. Drill and saw all the pieces at the
same time.

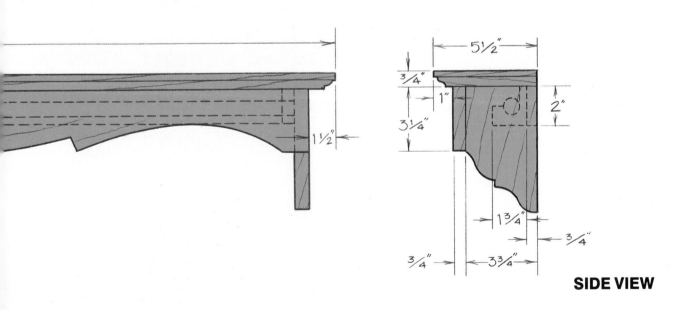

SIDE VIEW

5 Finish sand all parts.

Finish sand all parts. Finish sand all the parts of the window shelf. Make sure that you remove any remaining saw marks or mill marks. Be careful not to "break" or round over any edges where two parts join.

6 Assemble the window shelf.

Assemble the window shelf. Attach the sides, the front, and the cleat with glue and screws. Check that the assembly is square, then attach the top with glue and screws. Counterbore and counter- sink all the screws, then cover the heads with wooden plugs. Finally, glue the cleats to the inside surfaces of the sides, and clamp them in place until the glue dries.

7 Finish the window shelf.

Finish the window shelf. Remove any glue beads and finish sand any parts that may still need it. Sand the wooden plugs flush with the surfaces of the wood. "Break" all the exposed corners, rounding them over with a rasp and sandpaper to give them a soft, used appearance. Apply whatever stain or finish you prefer. We suggest you choose a finish to match the other wood trim or molding in the room where you intend to mount the window shelf.

8 Mount the window shelf.

Mount the window shelf. Use the cleat to mount the window shelf to the wall, by driving roundhead wood screws through the cleat and into the wall just above the window. In most homes, these screws will go through the drywall and bite into the frame header. (See Figure 1.) However, there is a chance that the wall will be hollow where you want to hang the project. If this is the case, use "Molly" anchors (also called hollow wall anchors) to mount the window shelf. (See Figure 2.) If you're mounting the project to a masonry wall, use expansion shields and lag screws. (See Figure 3.)

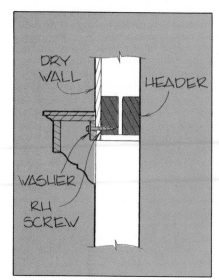

1/In most frame homes, you can drive ordinary roundhead wood screws *through* the cleat and into the window frame header.

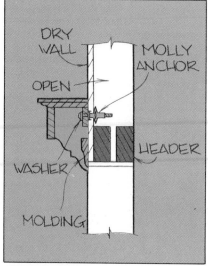

2/If the wall above the window is hollow, use Molly anchors *to* mount the window shelf.

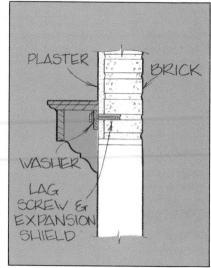

3/If you wish to mount the window shelf on a masonry wall, use lag screws *and* expansion shields.

Trestle Table and Benches

The trestle table was one of the earliest American country furniture designs. The reason for this is that it was the easiest table that a settler could make — just lay a wide plank over a sawbuck and presto! Instant table.

This sawbuck consisted of two crude, X-shaped assemblies or "trestles" joined by horizontal beams or stretchers. It was commonly used to hold logs so they could be sawn up into firewood. But it was so useful as a table support that the form persisted even after the settlers had the time to make more sophisticated tables.

Instead, they stylized the primitive sawbuck. The X-shaped trestles were filled in and cut into fancy shapes. The stretchers, too, were made more decorative. Eventually, the country form we know as the "trestle table" emerged.

The trestle table is also the earliest form of "knock-down" furniture. You can easily take it apart to store it or move it. The stretcher is mortised into the trestle and held in place by two wedges. To disassemble the table, remove the table top, knock the wedges loose, and take the stretcher and trestles apart. ⚙

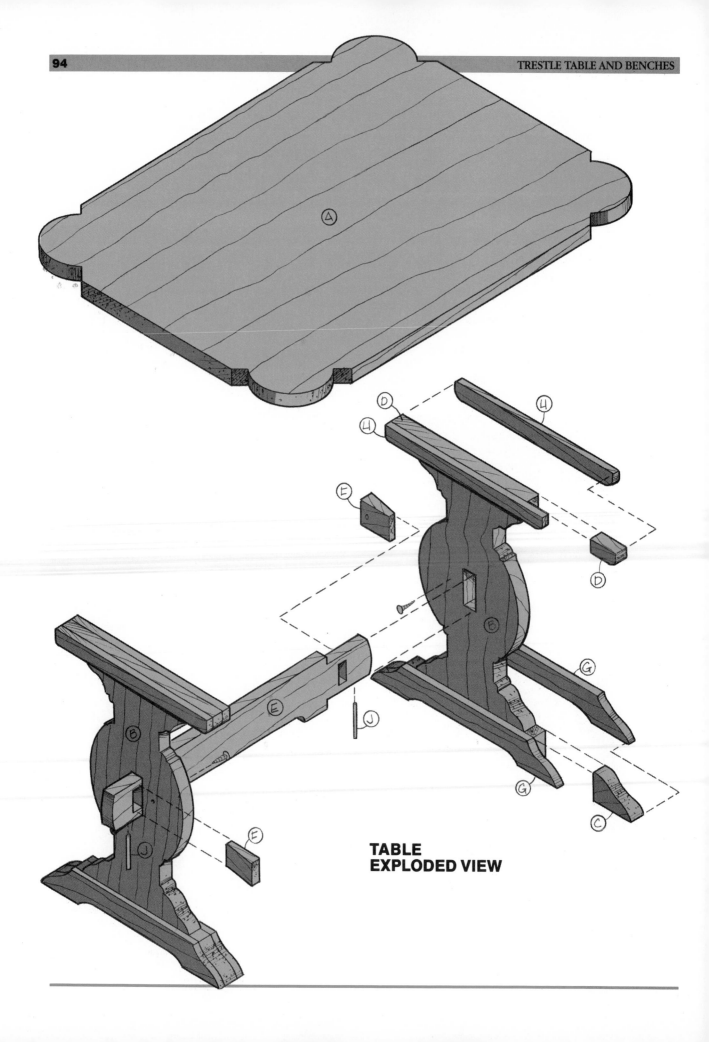

**TABLE
EXPLODED VIEW**

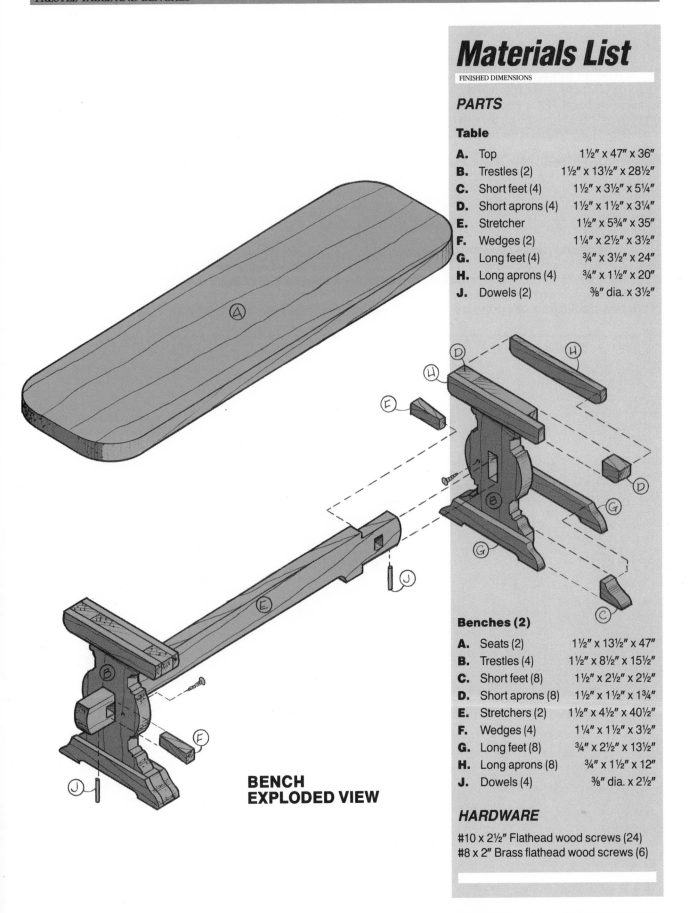

Materials List

FINISHED DIMENSIONS

PARTS

Table

A.	Top	1½″ x 47″ x 36″
B.	Trestles (2)	1½″ x 13½″ x 28½″
C.	Short feet (4)	1½″ x 3½″ x 5¼″
D.	Short aprons (4)	1½″ x 1½″ x 3¼″
E.	Stretcher	1½″ x 5¾″ x 35″
F.	Wedges (2)	1¼″ x 2½″ x 3½″
G.	Long feet (4)	¾″ x 3½″ x 24″
H.	Long aprons (4)	¾″ x 1½″ x 20″
J.	Dowels (2)	⅜″ dia. x 3½″

Benches (2)

A.	Seats (2)	1½″ x 13½″ x 47″
B.	Trestles (4)	1½″ x 8½″ x 15½″
C.	Short feet (8)	1½″ x 2½″ x 2½″
D.	Short aprons (8)	1½″ x 1½″ x 1¾″
E.	Stretchers (2)	1½″ x 4½″ x 40½″
F.	Wedges (4)	1¼″ x 1½″ x 3½″
G.	Long feet (8)	¾″ x 2½″ x 13½″
H.	Long aprons (8)	¾″ x 1½″ x 12″
J.	Dowels (4)	⅜″ dia. x 2½″

HARDWARE

#10 x 2½″ Flathead wood screws (24)
#8 x 2″ Brass flathead wood screws (6)

**BENCH
EXPLODED VIEW**

1

Adjust the design to your needs. As shown, the trestle table and benches will seat four adults comfortably — six, if you have a person pull up a chair at each end. If you want to seat more people, simply lengthen the table top, the bench seats, and the stretchers. Don't lengthen the table or the benches beyond 72″, however, without adding 1½″-thick, 3″-wide stiffeners beneath the top and seats to support the weight of extra people. These stiffeners should run lengthwise between the trestles.

Note: As you look over the working drawings, you'll notice that both the table and the benches are constructed exactly the same. The only difference is the size of the parts. For that reason, we suggest building them all at the same time. The following instructions are for *both* the table and the benches; we don't separate them.

2

Cut all the parts to size. To build this table, you'll need approximately 75 board feet of 8/4 ("eight-quarters") cabinet-grade lumber, planed to 1½″ thick; and approximately 8 board feet of 4/4 ("four-quarters") matching lumber, planed to ¾″ thick. Once you've selected and surfaced the wood, glue up the wide stock you'll need to make the table top, table trestles, and bench seats. Let the glue dry for at least 24 hours, and scrape the wide stock smooth. Then cut the parts to the sizes shown in the Materials List.

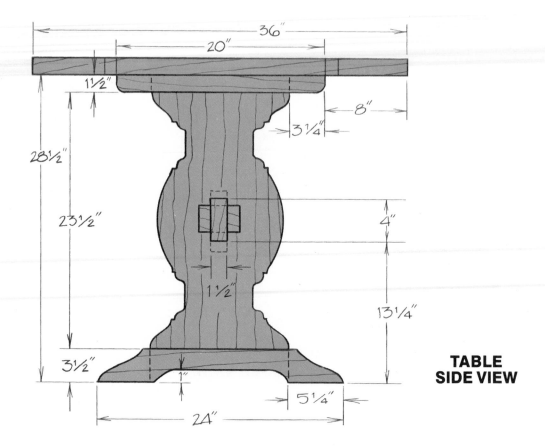

**TABLE
SIDE VIEW**

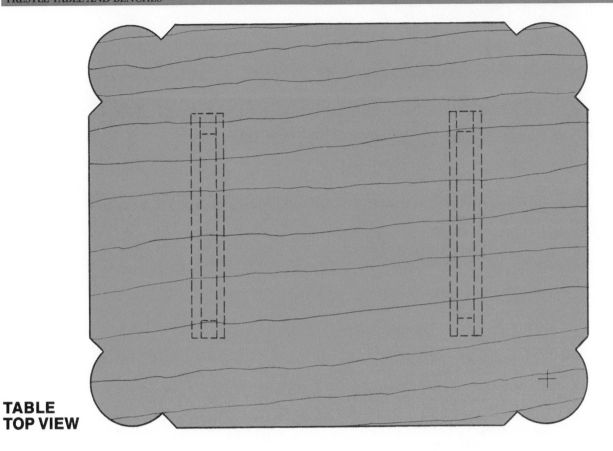

**TABLE
TOP VIEW**

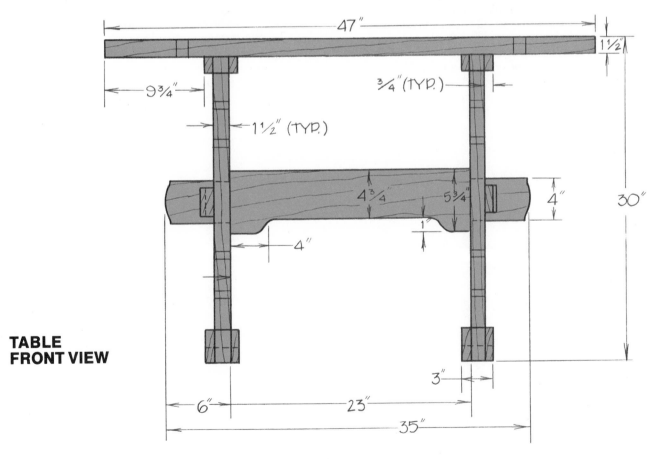

**TABLE
FRONT VIEW**

TRY THIS!   Because 8/4 cabinet-grade lumber is so expensive, and because much country furniture was traditionally built out of pine, you may be tempted to use construction-grade lumber to build this project. This is perfectly acceptable, particularly if you can find some good boards, but you must "cure" or dry the lumber before you use it. Cabinet lumber is dried to 7%–8% moisture content, while construction lumber is rarely dried to lower than 25%–30%. If you use the construction wood right away, parts of the project will shrink and warp. When selecting construction lumber to cure, pick boards with as few defects as possible. All the knots must be solid; discard any lumber with checks or splits. Purchase 25% more than you think you need. As the wood dries out, more defects will develop. Stack the wood *flat* with spacers in between each layer of boards, and let it sit inside your garage or shop for *at least* six months — preferably, a year. (A dry, unheated space is best for curing lumber.) This will bring the moisture content down to 10%–12%. It will never get as dry as kiln-dried cabinet-grade lumber, but it will cure adequately for most furniture projects.

3 Lay out the shapes of the parts and the locations of the mortises.

Enlarge the patterns for the trestles, stretchers, feet, and aprons, then trace the shapes on the stock. This is easier said than done, since there are quite a few patterns. For some time-saving tips, consult the section on *Enlarging Patterns*. Also, lay out the corners of the seats and table top. You won't need to enlarge patterns for these corners. They can be marked with a compass and a straightedge.

Note: When you lay out the patterns on the stock, pay careful attention to the grain direction. This is indicated on the *Table Trestle Pattern* and *Bench Trestle Pattern*. The grain direction is important for both the strength *and* the appearance of the trestles.

Before you cut the shapes of any parts, lay out the mortises on the trestles and stretchers as shown in the *Side Views* and *Stretcher Tenon Layouts*. It's much easier to measure the positions of these openings while the stock is still rectangular. After you cut the shapes, it will be almost impossible to place them accurately.

While you're laying out the mortises in the tenon-ends of the stretchers, note that these openings are positioned so that their inside edge is 1/16″ inside the mortise in the trestles. This is done so that when you tap the wedges in place, the wedges will hold the trestles tight against the tenon shoulders of the stretchers. If the stretcher mortise is outside the trestle mortise, the parts will remain loose no matter how tight you tap the wedges.

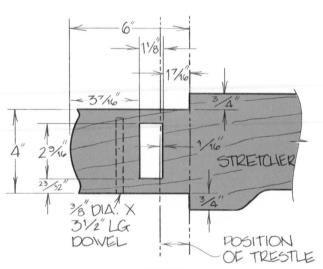

TABLE STRETCHER TENON LAYOUT

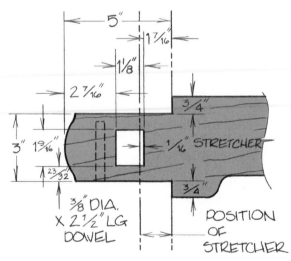

BENCH STRETCHER TENON LAYOUT

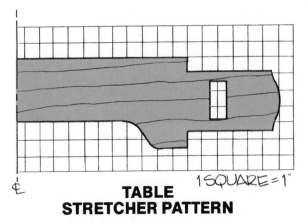

**TABLE
STRETCHER PATTERN**

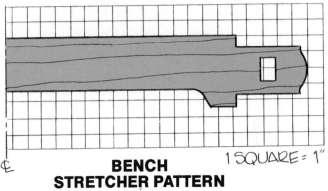

**BENCH
STRETCHER PATTERN**

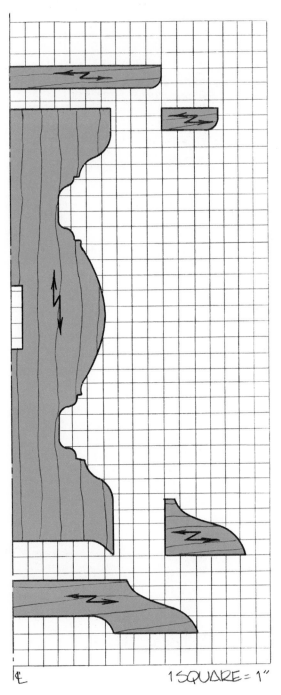

**TABLE
TRESTLE PATTERN**

**BENCH
TRESTLE
PATTERN**

4 **Cut the shapes of the parts.** After you've laid out all the patterns, corners, and mortises, cut the outside shapes of the parts. You can use a variety of tools to do this — sabre saw, scroll saw, and band saw. But you'll probably find the sabre saw is the one tool that will do all the cutting. The table top and seats, for instance, are much too large to cut on a scroll saw or band saw, so a sabre saw is essential. You can use a band saw to cut the shapes of the stretchers and table trestles, but some of the curves on the seat trestle are positioned so that you can't get at them with a band saw that you'd normally find in a home workshop. So cut away as much stock as you can with the band saw, then switch to the scroll saw to finish up. But again, a sabre saw will manage all these cuts if you excercise patience and care.

Whatever tool you use, remember this is thick stock. Take it easy. If you force the work, the blades will heat up and break — particularly sabre saw and scroll saw blades.

Note: In most furniture projects, it's standard practice to cut the joinery, *then* shape the parts. The trestle table is the exception to the rule. The mortises do not require

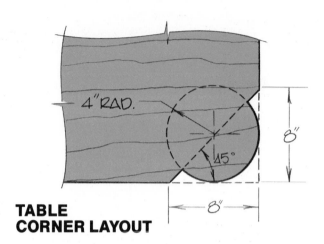

TABLE CORNER LAYOUT

that the boards have a straight edge to cut them accurately, as long as you lay the mortises out before you cut the shapes. And the trestle stock, because it's so thick, is heavy and cumbersome. By cutting the shapes of the trestles first you remove a great deal of stock, making the workpieces easier to handle.

5 **Cut the mortises.** The waste in the mortises must be cut away without cutting through from the outside edge. To do this, use a sabre saw technique called internal cutting or, sometimes, "piercing."

To make an internal cut with a sabre saw, first drill a ½"-diameter hole inside the waste area that you want to cut away. When cutting out a small rectangular area — as in the case of these mortises — it's sometimes easier to

drill *four* holes, one at each corner. Remember, the holes may butt up to the line, but none of them should stray out of the waste area. (See Figure 1.) Insert the blade of the jigsaw through one of the holes and saw along the line to the next hole. Repeat until you have cut all four sides of the mortise. (See Figure 2.) Remove the waste, then go back and square up the corners with the saw.

*1/*To cut the mortises, first drill holes in all four corners. Back up the wood when you drill these holes, so there's no tear-out where the drill bit exits.

*2/*Insert the sabre saw blade in the holes and cut along the lines. Take it very slow, especially when cutting with the grain. If you go too fast, the blade will heat up and break. It may also "cup" in the wood, trying to follow the annual rings — the path of least resistance. If this happens, you won't get a square mortise.

TRY THIS! To get the stretcher tenon to fit snugly in the mortise, cut just inside the marked line. Then "hand-fit" the tenon to the mortise, cutting away just a little stock at a time with a file or rasp until you get the fit you want. Don't make the fit *too* snug.

Remember, the finish will likely add a few hundredths of an inch to the thickness of the tenon. That doesn't sound like much, but it's enough to make a tight fit into no fit at all.

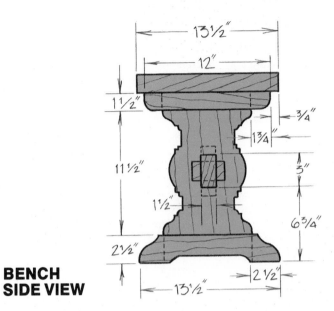

**BENCH
SIDE VIEW**

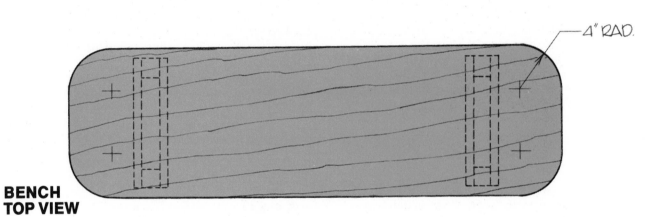

**BENCH
TOP VIEW**

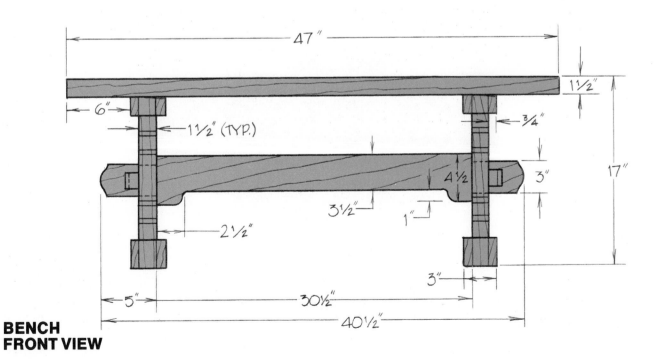

**BENCH
FRONT VIEW**

6

Reinforce the stretcher mortises. The stretcher mortises are vulnerable to splitting out, particularly if you tap the wedges in too tightly. To prevent this, reinforce the outside wall of the mortises with ⅜" dowels, as shown in the *Stretcher Layouts*. Drill ⅜"-diameter stopped holes for these dowels from the *underside* of the stretcher tenons. Coat the dowels with glue and tap them in place. When the glue cures, sand off the dowels flush with the surface of the wood.

7

Assemble the trestles, feet, and aprons. Finish sand the faces of the trestle to get it ready for assembly. Don't bother to sand the edges just yet.

Glue the short feet and short aprons to the trestles. Let the glue set up for a few minutes — long enough to get some "tack" — then glue the long feet and long aprons to this assembly. (The tack that develops after a few minutes keeps the small parts from shifting while you add the larger parts.) Clamp the assembly and let the glue cure thoroughly, for at least 24 hours.

8

Sand the cut edges. When the glue dries, sand the saw marks from the cut edges of the trestle assemblies. (A 1" belt sander or "strip" sander, as it's sometimes called, works well for this operation.) "True up" the aprons and feet, so that the edges of the sandwiched parts are perfectly even. When you've finished sanding them, they should look like one solid block of wood attached to the top and the bottom of the trestles.

Sand the saw marks from the corners of the table top and the bench seats. Round over the edges of these parts so that they will be comfortable to use.

9

Make and fit the wedges. Using a band saw, taper the wedges as shown in the *Wedge Section*. Sand the saw marks from the cut surfaces of the wedges. Dry-assemble the stretchers and the trestles, then test-fit the wedges in the stretcher mortises. If necessary, pare the wedges down until you're satisfied with the fit.

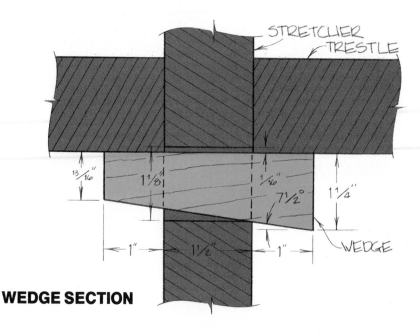

WEDGE SECTION

10 Assemble the tables and benches.

Tap the wedges in place, then drive brass flat-head wood screws through the trestles from the inside surface, into the wedge, as shown in the *Mortise & Tenon Assemblies*. These screws keep the wedges tight in the mortises. The brass is less noticeable against a dark- or medium-colored wood. Countersink the screws, but don't cover the heads. That way, should you ever want to disassemble the table, all you have to do is remove the screws.

Attach the tops and seats to the trestle/stretcher assemblies with flathead wood screws. (They don't have to be brass.) Drive these screws through the aprons and into the underside of the top and seats, where they will never be seen. Once again, countersink the screws but don't cover the heads.

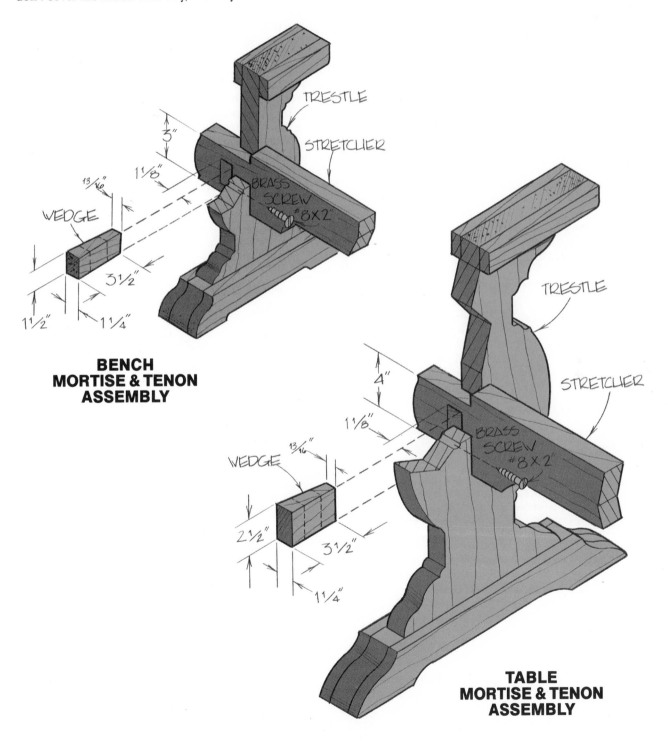

BENCH MORTISE & TENON ASSEMBLY

TABLE MORTISE & TENON ASSEMBLY

11 Finish the individual parts and assemblies.

Disassemble the tables and benches completely, removing all screws. Finish sand the parts, then apply a finish to them. Be careful to coat each surface of each part or assembly the same number of times, whether it will be seen or not. If one side of one part has fewer coats than another side, it will absorb and release moisture at a faster rate. This will cause the part to warp.

If you wish, stencil the top of the table and the benches. This should be done *before* you apply the final finish. Consult the section on *Stenciling* to familiarize yourself with the basic techniques, then cut the templates needed. You can either design your own stencil pattern, or follow the patterns shown here. To stencil these patterns, you'll need to cut three templates per pattern — one for the border, one for the flower petals and buds, and one for the leaves and the middle of the flower. (See Figure 3.)

Align the templates by cutting four small, triangular shapes near the outer edges. Stack up the templates in a "pad," carefully lining up the shape; then cut all the tri-angles at once. This way, the triangles will all be positioned exactly the same on each template. When you attach the first stencil to the wood, put a piece of masking tape under the registration triangles, and trace the shape of the triangles with a marker. Using the tape will keep you from marking the wood. (See Figure 4.) When you're ready to position the next template, simply line up its registration triangles with the marks on the tape.

The stencil you see here was done with acrylic paint, applied directly to the raw wood, then covered with a medium-to-light varnish stain. This dulled the bright colors of the stencil, and gave it an antique look. It also imbedded the stencil in a hard varnish coat, so that it won't wear off easily.

If you prefer the bright colors, first stain the wood with any ordinary penetrating stain, then seal the stain in the wood with a coat of sanding sealer. The sealer prevents the oils in the stain from mixing with the pigments in the paints and dulling them, and likewise prevents the oils from clouding the final finish. Stencil the stained, sealed wood, then cover the entire project with a clear varnish or polyurethane finish.

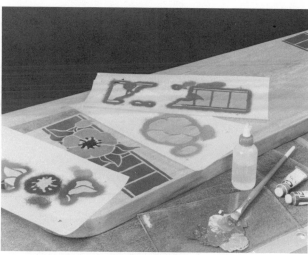

3/To stencil the table top and seats, cut three templates per pattern — one for the blue portions of the design, one for the violet, and one for the green and black. The templates you see here are cut from a thin plastic film called Mylar. It's available at most art supply and drafting supply stores.

4/Cut identical triangles in each of the templates to help align them on the wood. Affix a piece of tape to the wood to mark each triangle, so that you won't have to mark it directly on the wood.

12 Assemble the finished table and benches.

Rub down the completed finish with a hard paste wax. Also, apply a generous amount of wax *inside* the mortises. With the inside surfaces waxed, you will be able to push tenons and the wedges through the mortises without scratching the finish on the tenons or the wedges. Reassemble all the parts.

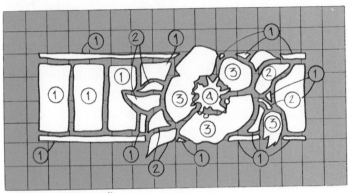

1 SQUARE = 1"

STENCIL PATTERN FOR BENCH

▨ OVERLAP
FOR POSITION

COLORS:
1. BLUE
2. GREEN
3. VIOLET
4. CHARCOAL
   BROWN

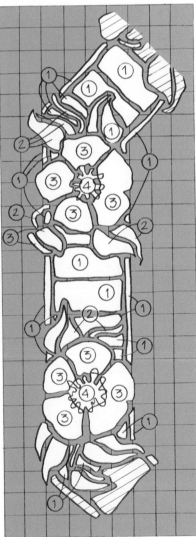

**STENCIL
PATTERN
FOR TABLE**

1 SQUARE = 1"

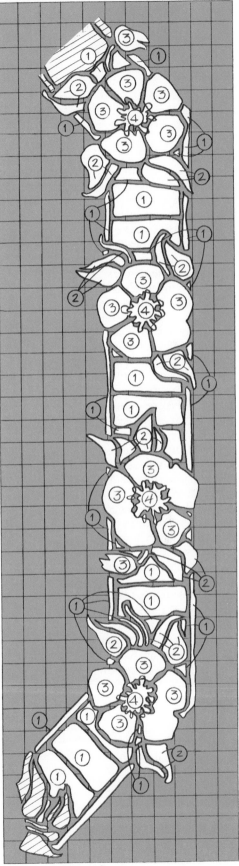

1 SQUARE = 1"

Pouting Chair

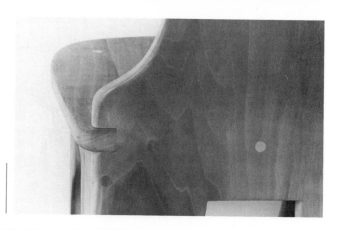

Many of us remember, as children, being sent to "sit in the corner" when we misbehaved. There was often a chair or stool in this unlucky corner, where we would plop down and think about our misdeeds. Our fathers and grandfathers occupied similar stools in similar corners when they were young — under similar circumstances. The custom was so pervasive in this country that after a time, these stools became known as "pouting chairs."

How did these stools get in these corners? That's another story: The pouting chair had another purpose, long before it was used as a form of punishment. It evolved from the simple step-stool. At some forgotten moment in our past, an inventive country woodworker decided to attach a long handle to his stool, so that he wouldn't constantly have to bend over to move it. The stool-plus-handle combination looked like a child's chair with an exceptionally high back. This innovation caught on, and highback stools began to appear in many country homes. They were usually stored in some out-of-the-way corner — the same corner where an errant child would be sent.

Today, the pouting chair remains just as useful as it ever was — for *both* its applications. The stool you see here is decorated with some traditional country fretwork. The legs are folk imitations of the classic cabriole shape, and the back is pierced with a wildflower design.

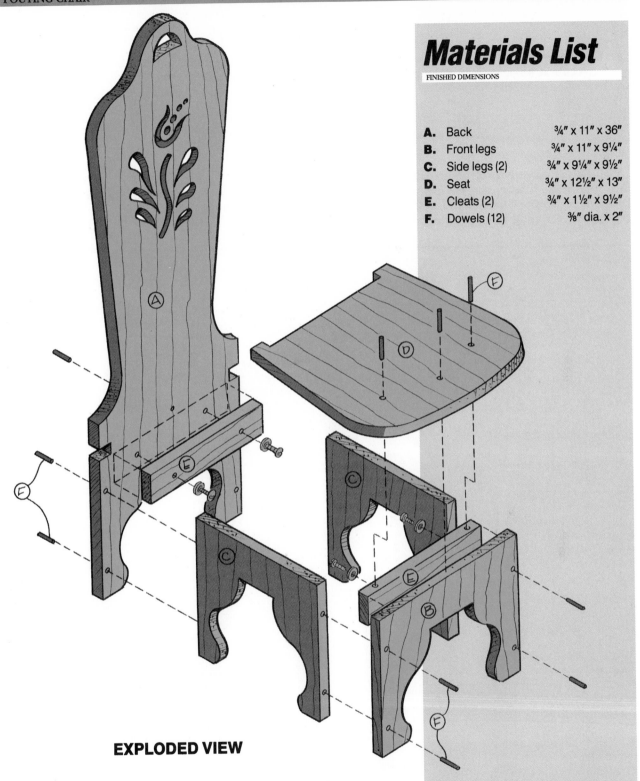

Materials List

FINISHED DIMENSIONS

A.	Back	¾″ x 11″ x 36″
B.	Front legs	¾″ x 11″ x 9¼″
C.	Side legs (2)	¾″ x 9¼″ x 9½″
D.	Seat	¾″ x 12½″ x 13″
E.	Cleats (2)	¾″ x 1½″ x 9½″
F.	Dowels (12)	⅜″ dia. x 2″

EXPLODED VIEW

HARDWARE

#10 x 1¼″ Roundhead wood screws and
  washers (4)

1 **Cut the parts to size.** You can make this project from a single 1 x 12, 8′ long. (In fact, you will have a foot or so left over.) Glue up the 13″-wide stock you need for the seat, then cut the stock to the sizes shown in the Materials List.

2 **Cut the seat-to-back joinery.** Cut two ¾″-wide, ¾″-deep notches in both edges of the back, where shown on the *Front View* and *Back/Front Leg Pattern*. Cut another notch centered in the back edge of the seat, 9½″ wide and ¾″ deep, as shown in the *Top View*. All of these notches must fit together. The fit should be snug, but not too tight.

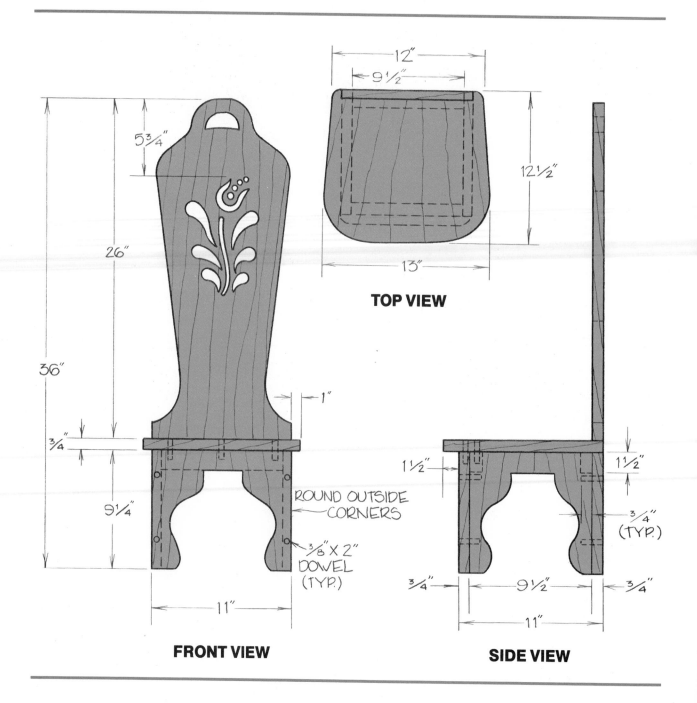

TOP VIEW

FRONT VIEW

SIDE VIEW

3 **Cut the outside shapes of the back and legs.** Enlarge the *Seat Pattern,* the *Side Leg Pattern,* the *Fretwork Pattern* and the *Back/Front Leg Pattern.* Trace these patterns onto the respective boards. With a band saw or a sabre saw, cut the outside shapes of the back, front legs, and side legs. Sand away the saw marks from the cut edges.

TRY THIS! Instead of going to the trouble of making cardboard or hardboard templates to transfer the patterns, simply tape carbon paper to the stock, carbon side down. Tape the enlarged paper pattern on top of the carbon paper, and trace the pattern lines with a ballpoint pen.

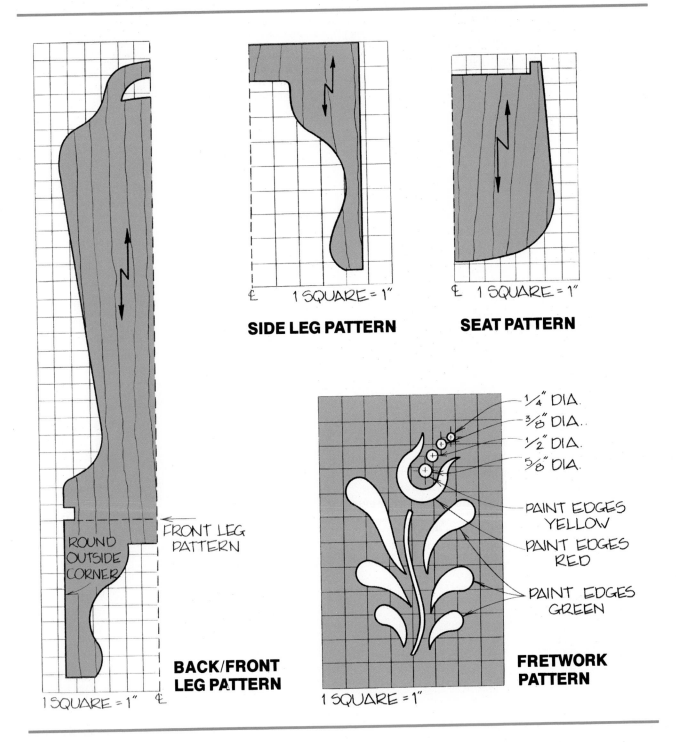

SIDE LEG PATTERN

1 SQUARE = 1"

SEAT PATTERN

1 SQUARE = 1"

ROUND OUTSIDE CORNER

FRONT LEG PATTERN

BACK/FRONT LEG PATTERN

1 SQUARE = 1"

¼" DIA.
⅜" DIA.
½" DIA.
⅝" DIA.

PAINT EDGES YELLOW

PAINT EDGES RED

PAINT EDGES GREEN

FRETWORK PATTERN

1 SQUARE = 1"

4 **Drill and cut the handle and the fretwork design.** Cut the interior shape of the fretwork wildflower design in the back by making a series of "piercing cuts" with your sabre saw. (The back is too large for you to make these cuts on a jigsaw or scroll saw.) Drill a ½"-diameter hole through the stock where you want to cut an interior shape. This hole must be made in the *waste* that you wish to cut out. Insert the sabre saw blade in the hole, then cut out from the hole to the pattern cutlines. (See Figure 1.) Cut out the waste, and sand the interior cut edges to remove the saw marks.

The top part of the flower (the pistil, for you gardeners) can be created with a drill alone. There's no need to saw any shapes. Drill four holes through the stock, each a different diameter — ¼", ⅜", ½", and ⅝", as shown on the *Fretwork Design.*

1/To make a piercing cut, first drill a hole in the waste area. Insert the blade of the saw through the hole and saw out to the pattern line. Choose a fine blade for this work, with many "teeth per inch." This will give you a smoother cut, and the cut edge of the fretwork will require less sanding.

5 **Round the edges of the legs.** Round over the outside corner of the front legs and the back (below the notches), where shown on the *Front View* and *Back/Front Leg Pattern.* Use a router and a *piloted* ½"-radius quarter-round bit. Be careful not to rout any adjoining surfaces.

6 **Finish sand all parts.** Finish sand all the parts of the chair, with the exception of the cleats. Make sure that you remove any remaining saw marks or mill marks. Be careful not to "break" or round over any edges or surfaces where two parts join.

7 **Assemble the chair.** Attach the cleats to the back and the front leg with roundhead wood screws and washers. *Use no glue.* Drill oversize pilot holes for the screws, to allow the back and the front leg to expand and contract with changes in humidity.

Assemble the back, front legs, and side legs with glue, then reinforce the glue joints with dowels. After the glue on this assembly sets up, put the seat in place and attach it to the chair with dowels. *Do not* glue the seat to the cleats or side legs, although you should glue the dowels in place. Rely on the dowels and the seat-to-back joinery to keep the seat in place.

TRY THIS! Instead of dowels, you can use flathead wood screws. Counterbore and countersink the screws, then cover the heads with wooden plugs.

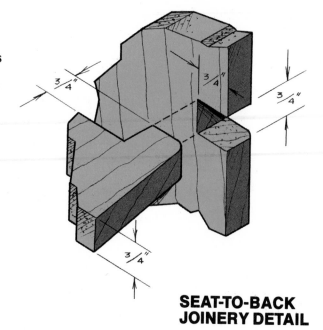

3/4" 3/4" 3/4" 3/4"

SEAT-TO-BACK JOINERY DETAIL

8 **Finish the chair.** Remove any glue beads and finish sand any parts that may still need it. "Break" all the exposed corners, rounding them over with a rasp and sandpaper to give them a worn appearance.

Paint the *interior* edges of the wildflower fretwork design. (See Figure 2.) *Do not* paint the face surface of the back. By painting just the edges, the shape of the wild-flower will appear in color every time you view the flower from an angle. Color the leaves and the stem green, the petals red, and the pistil yellow, as shown in the *Fretwork Design*. Use an acrylic or a latex paint.

After the paint on the fretwork design dries, apply a clear penetrating oil finish, such as Danish oil or tung oil, to the entire chair. Avoid coating finishes, such as varnish or polyurethane. These finishes have to be rubbed out, and you'll find that the fretwork makes this hard to do.

2/Paint just the interior edges of the fretwork, using a fine brush. If you get any paint on the face surface of the back, sand it off after the paint dries.

Artificial Patina

When a piece of furniture sits around for a hundred years, the surface of the wood takes on a warm glow. A slow reaction with the oxygen in the air changes the color of the wood, making it appear darker and richer. When this happens, we say that the piece has developed a "patina." A deep, well cared-for patina adds greatly to the value of an antique — or a reproduction.

You can speed up this chemical reaction with a catalyst, nitric acid (HNO_3). This acid, when properly applied, creates an "artificial patina" on your reproduction that is almost indistinguishable from the real thing. It also brings out burls, bird's-eyes, and curly grain patterns, giving the light and dark areas of the wood grain more contrast. Two projects in this book — the "Pouting Chair" and the "Spice Chest" — have been treated with acid to make them appear well-aged.

Nitric acid is available through most chemical supply houses. Although it is not a controlled substance, it is very dangerous and *must be used with extreme caution.* Wear a long-sleeve shirt, long pants, rubber gloves, and a *full-face mask* when mixing and applying the acid. Work out-of-doors; the acid gives off toxic fumes as it works on the wood. Keep a running garden hose nearby, just in case you spill or splash acid on you. Store the acid in a dark place — it reacts with light.

In a glass container, mix full-strength nitric acid 1:5 with distilled water to make a 20% solution. Using an old paint brush, wet down a small area (about 2 square feet) of your project with the acid solution. Let this soak in for a few seconds, then heat the surface of the wood with a heat gun. As the wood heats up, the patina will "develop," just like the image on a photograph. (See Figure A.) Repeat this procedure until you have created a patina over your entire project. Don't worry about overlapping areas; they won't show.

Immediately after you complete the patina, neutralize the acid in the wood. Sponge on a light application of household ammonia. Do this at an arm's length; the surface of the wood will give off dingy yellow fumes that you *don't* want to breathe. When you have neutralized the entire surface, let it sit in a sheltered area (garage, carport, storage barn) to dry for several days. *Don't* bring it inside your house or shop to dry. The project will continue to give off fumes until the ammonia is completely evaporated.

When the project is dry, give it a light sanding with very fine sandpaper. If you wish, sand the corners and edges a little harder than other areas to make the patina appear lighter at these points. This will imitate the natural wear that would have taken place if the project were a hundred years old, making the patina more realistic.

A/After applying the acid, heat the surface with a heat gun to "develop" the patina. Keep the gun moving so as not to burn the wood. And be patient. It takes a little while for the patina to develop. Practice this on a few scraps before you "patina-ize" your project.

Candle Sconce

Here's an interesting bit of trivia: "Sconce" is descended from an old Dutch word, "schans," which means a fortress or shelter. The "candle sconce" was a shelter for the candle, a tiny three-sided fortress to keep the flame safe from the wind.

Candles and candle sconces were once an essential part of country life, more precious than we can imagine in this electrified age. A Colonial doctor, writing in the early 1700s, recorded his impressions of a celebration at the Governor's Palace in Williamsburg, Virginia. What impressed him most was "a magnificent display" of light. The Governor had lit *seven* candles. The candle was the colonists' best defense against the night, and the sconce was the candle's best protection.

Some sconces, like the one you see here, were designed to be more effective than protective. The sides were lowered and the backs were inset with polished metal or a mirror to throw more light into the room. Sconces such as these were rarely carried from place to place, since there was little to shield the flame from sudden drafts. Instead, they were hung permanently on a wall — the same way we hang lamps and light fixtures today.

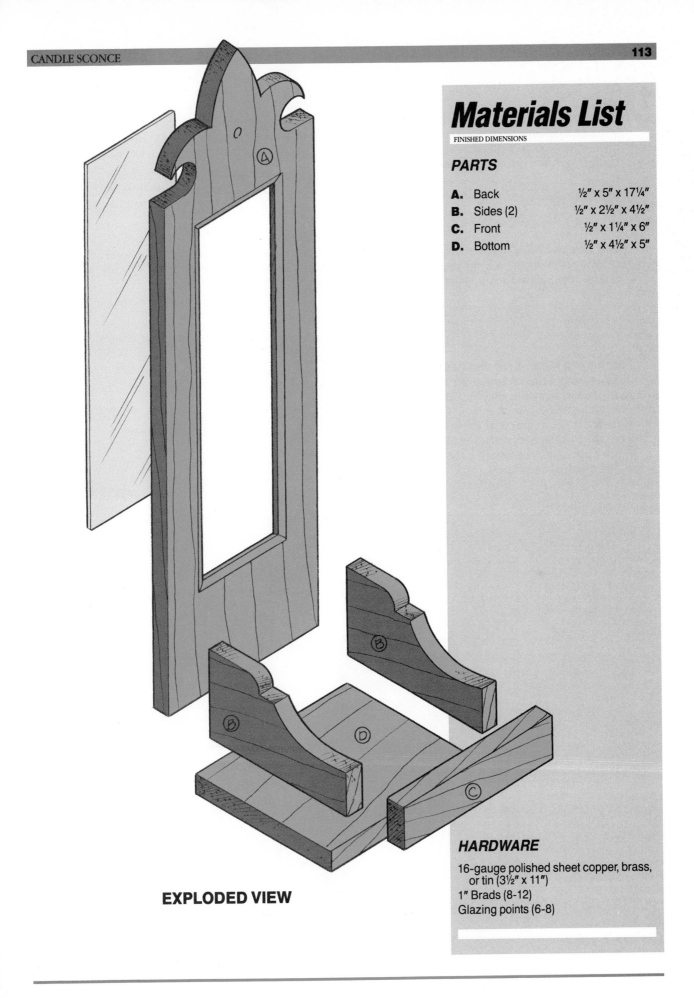

Materials List

FINISHED DIMENSIONS

PARTS

A.	Back	½" x 5" x 17¼"
B.	Sides (2)	½" x 2½" x 4½"
C.	Front	½" x 1¼" x 6"
D.	Bottom	½" x 4½" x 5"

HARDWARE

16-gauge polished sheet copper, brass, or tin (3½" x 11")
1" Brads (8-12)
Glazing points (6-8)

EXPLODED VIEW

1

Cut the parts to size. Plane the ½"-thick stock you'll need for this project. If you don't have a planer, several mail-order woodworking companies sell stock of various thicknesses. You can also have the stock planed for a small fee at most lumberyards or millwork shops. Once you have the stock planed to the proper thickness, cut the parts to the sizes shown in the Materials List.

2

Cut the opening for the reflector. The reflector opening is made by "piercing" the back stock. Mark the opening as shown in the *Front View*, then drill a ½"-diameter hole in the waste. Insert the blade of a sabre saw in the hole, and saw out from the hole to the cutlines.

3

Make the rabbet for the reflector. Mount a *piloted* rabbeting bit in your router, and mount your router in a router table. (If you don't have a router table, make sure that the stock is clamped securely to your workbench before you start to cut.) Cut a ¼"-wide, ¼"-deep rabbet in the back surface of the back, all around the reflector opening. (See Figure 1.) Square the corners of the rabbet with a hand chisel.

1/Use a router mounted to a router table to cut the rabbet for the metal reflector. If you use the router alone, you have to clamp the stock to the edge of the table so that the piloted bit won't hit the table. This usually requires that you shift the workpiece several times as you cut.

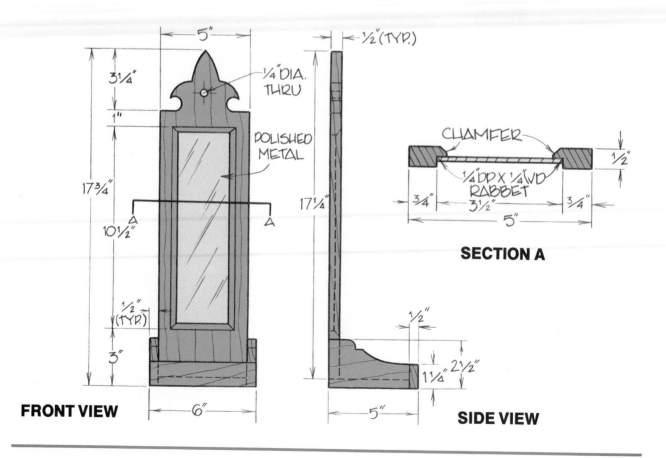

FRONT VIEW

SIDE VIEW

SECTION A

4 Chamfer the front of the reflector opening.

Replace the rabbeting bit with a piloted chamfering bit. (See Figure 2.) Turn the back stock over so that the front side faces up, and rout a chamfer around the edge of the reflector opening, as shown in *Section A*. With a flat chisel, finish the chamfers at the corners, where the bit won't reach. (See Figure 3.)

Note: The chamfering is optional. You could also cut a bead, cove, ogee, or any shape that you prefer. You may also leave the edge square.

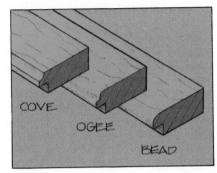

2/To "frame" the reflector, chamfer the front edge of the reflector opening with a piloted chamfer router bit. You can also rout a bead, cove, or ogee. Shown here are several options.

3/Carve the chamfer in the corners, where the bit won't reach. This is fairly simple for a chamfer, but it gets a bit tricky if you've elected to make a bead, a cove, or an ogee.

5 Cut the shapes of the back and sides.

Enlarge the patterns for the top portion of the back and the top edge of the sides. Trace the patterns on the stock, then cut out the shapes with a band saw, scroll saw, or sabre saw. If you wish to hang this project from a nail, drill a ¼"-diameter hole near the top of the back, where shown in the *Top Pattern*.

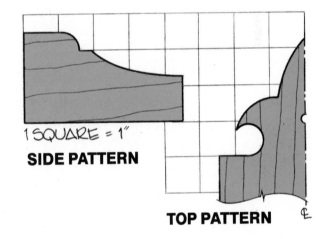

1 SQUARE = 1"

SIDE PATTERN

TOP PATTERN

6 Finish sand the parts.

Remove the saw marks from the sawn edges with rasps or sandpaper. Then finish sand all the parts to get them ready for assembly.

7 Assemble the candle sconce.

Apply glue to all the adjoining surfaces, and clamp the parts together while the glue sets. After the glue has set, reinforce the glue joints with brads.

8 Finish the candle sconce.

Do any necessary touch-up sanding to the sconce. While you're at it, "break" the hard corners of the stock with sandpaper, rounding them over slightly. This will give the sconce a worn appearance. Apply a finish or a stain. When this dries, set the sheet metal reflector in the rabbet, and fasten it in place with glazing points.

Hutch

The hutch was one of the most necessary pieces of furniture in the country kitchen. The curious name comes from an old English word, *hucche,* meaning a storage bin. The hutch was where the cook stored almost everything that she needed to prepare and serve food — dishes, mixing bowls, cooking and eating utensils of all descriptions.

There are a variety of hutch designs. Each new wave of immigrants brought with them the memories of similar kitchen storage cabinets that they left behind. When they built new hutches, they blended their own furniture traditions with other designs that they found here. Consequently, it's hard to find two country hutches exactly the same. The hutch pictured here is perhaps the most typical — closed cabinet below, open shelves above, and counter space in the middle.

This particular country hutch is a simple piece to build, considering it's such a large piece of furniture. The craftsman who made it probably had nothing more than ordinary eighteenth-century carpenter's tools. So he used only basic joinery — dadoes, rabbets, grooves, and pegs. Even the shaped edge of the top and the counter is just a chamfer cut with a block plane.

Despite its simplicity — or because of it — the hutch has an elegance and a warmth that will add character to any country kitchen. It's a solid wood-working design, too, as evidenced by the fact that this piece of furniture is still serviceable after nearly 200 years. It's safe to say that your family will enjoy it for generations. ❀

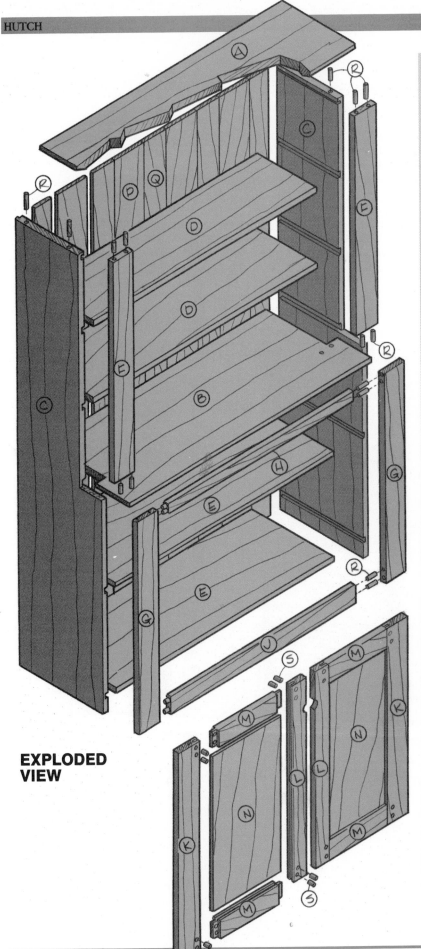

EXPLODED VIEW

Materials List

FINISHED DIMENSIONS

PARTS

A.	Top	1¼" x 13¼" x 45½"
B.	Countertop	1¼" x 17⅜" x 45½"
C.	Sides (2)	¾" x 15¾" x 70¾"
D.	Upper shelves (2)	¾" x 10⅞" x 42¼"
E.	Lower shelves (2)	¾" x 15⅜" x 42¼"
F.	Upper stiles (2)	¾" x 4" x 35¾"
G.	Face frame stiles (2)	¾" x 4" x 33¾"
H.	Upper face frame rail	¾" x 1½" x 35"
J.	Lower face frame rail	¾" x 3" x 35"
K.	Outside door frame stiles (2)	¾" x 4" x 29⅛"
L.	Inside door frame stiles (2)	¾" x 2½" x 29⅛"
M.	Door frame rails (4)	¾" x 3" x 12⅜"
N.	Door frame panels (2)	¼" x 12¼" x 23½"
P.	Wide back boards (4)	⅜" x 5⅞" x 68⅞"
Q.	Narrow back boards (5)	⅜" x 3⅝" x 68⅞"
R.	Dowels (24)	⅜" dia. x 2"
S.	Pegs (16)	¼" dia. x ¾"

HARDWARE

1½" x 2½" Butt hinges and mounting screws (2 pairs)
Bullet catches and striker plates (2 sets)
6d Cut nails (1 lb.)
4d Finishing nails (½ lb.)

1

Cut the parts to size. To build this project, you'll need approximately 62 board feet of cabinet-grade lumber, total. Purchase 46 feet of 4/4 (four-quarters) lumber, and plane 32 board feet to ¾" thick. Resaw the rest of the 4/4 stock, splitting it in half on your band saw. Then plane 5 _square_ feet of the resawn boards (enough to make the door panels) to ¼" thick, and the rest to ⅜" thick.

You'll also need 16 board feet of 6/4 (six-quarters) lumber, planed to 1¼" thick. 6/4 is hard to find, but some large suppliers of cabinet woods will either have it on hand, or place a special order for you. In a pinch, purchase 8/4 lumber, then resaw it and plane it to make 1¼"-thick _and_ ⅜"-thick stock.

Glue up the wide stock you need to make the top, countertop, door panels, and bottom shelves. The side stock needs to be glued up as well, but you can save yourself some time by cutting the parts to size before you glue them edge to edge. Cut two boards for each side, one board ¾" x 11¼" x 70¾", and the other ¾" x 4½" x 33¾". Glue these up to make the L-shaped sides.

Cut the rest of the parts to the sizes shown in the Materials List. If you wish, make the door frame parts slightly oversize from what is shown. After you assemble them, you can plane the doors down to get a perfect fit. Remember that you must increase both the length _and_ the width of the rails and stiles ⅛"-¼" to be able to do this.

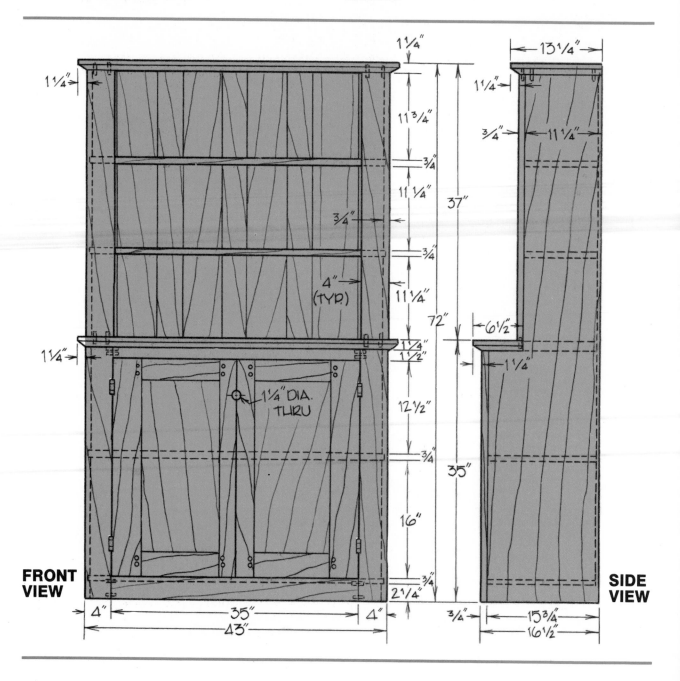

FRONT VIEW

SIDE VIEW

2 Cut the joinery in the sides.

Rout ¾"-wide, ⅜"-deep dadoes and a 1"-wide, ⅜"-deep dado in the inside surface of the sides, where shown in the *Side Layout*. Use a straightedge clamped to the side to guide your router. (See Figure 1.) Using a piloted rabbeting bit or an edge guide, rout a ⅜"-wide, ⅜"-deep rabbet along the back edge of the sides and the top. Note that the rabbet in the top is blind at both ends, as shown in the *Top Layout*.

Make each dado or rabbet in several passes, cutting ⅛" deeper with each pass. Square the blind ends of the rabbet in the top with a hand chisel.

1/A T-shaped jig — really, just a large T-square — makes it simple to rout dadoes and grooves in wide stock. Use the cross of the T to align the jig, and the leg as a straightedge to guide the router.

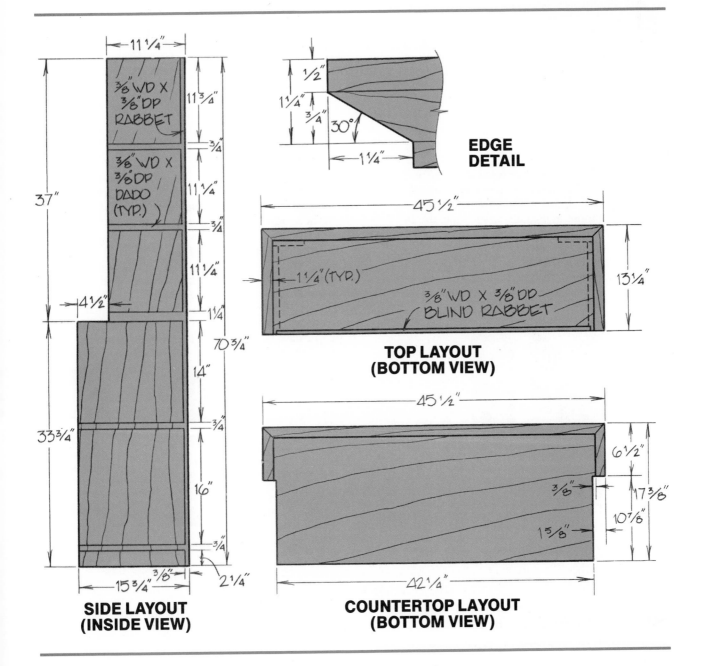

EDGE DETAIL

TOP LAYOUT (BOTTOM VIEW)

SIDE LAYOUT (INSIDE VIEW)

COUNTERTOP LAYOUT (BOTTOM VIEW)

3 **Make the chamfer in the top and countertop.** Attach a tall (8″-high or more) fence extension to the rip fence of your table saw. This will help support the wide stock and keep it square to the blade. Tilt the blade (or your table) to 30°, and cut a chamfer in the front and side edges of the top and the countertop. (See Figure 2.) Smooth the chamfer, removing the saw marks, with a block plane and a scraper.

Option: If you wish, you can cut other shapes besides the chamfer. Using your router or a shaper, make an ogee, cove, bead or some other shape of your own choosing.

2/A wide fence extension, bolted to your rip fence, aids in cutting the chamfer. Use a hollow-ground planer blade to make the cut. This will leave a smooth surface that requires little scraping or sanding.

4 **Cut the shape of the countertop.** Lay out the shape of the countertop. As shown in the *Countertop Layout,* the counter is T-shaped, with two "wings" on either side. Cut the shape with a sabre saw or a hand saw.

Option: While you've got your sabre saw out, you may wish to shape other parts. The upper stiles can be scalloped to add decoration to the hutch. Notches can be cut in the front edges of the upper shelves to hold spoons and other utensils.

5 **Cut the door frame joinery.** The door frame is assembled with pinned tongue-and-groove joints. Note that the grooves in the stiles are deeper than those in the rails, as shown in the *Door Joinery Detail.* The deeper groove accommodates the tongues on the ends of the rails.

Using a router or a dado cutter, cut the ¼″-wide, ⅜″-deep grooves in the rails first. Readjust the depth

of cut, and cut the grooves in the stiles. Finally, cut the tongues in the rails. Usually, these tongues are made with a circular saw blade. But if you're using a dado cutter to cut the grooves, you can use the same setup to make the tongues. Hold the rails square to the cutter with a tenoning jig. (See Figure 3.)

Clamp the two middle door stiles together, edge to edge. Drill a 1¼″-diameter hole between them, near the upper end, as shown in the *Front View.* This hole will serve as a finger pull for the doors.(The original hutch has no door pulls of any sort. For two hundred years, people have been breaking their fingernails to get the doors open!)

DOOR PANEL

¼″WD X ¾″ DP DADO

¼″WD X ¼″DP DADO

¼″DIA. X ¾″LG. PEG

¾″

¼″

2¾″

2½″

3″

¾″

DOOR JOINERY DETAIL

3/Use a tenoning jig to hold the rails when cutting the tongues. This jig rides along the fence, and holds long stock straight up and down.

6 **Finish sand all parts.** Finish sand all the parts of the hutch, carefully removing any planer marks or saw marks. Be careful not to round over any corners or edges that join other parts.

7

Join the parts of the face frame. Using a doweling jig to guide your drill, bore dowel holes to join the face frame rails and stile. "Dry assemble" the parts with dowels, to test the fit. If you're satisfied that the parts fit properly, glue the frame together.

TRY THIS! There are several alternatives for joining face frame members. Among them: (1) You can use lap joints. You'll be able to see the end grain of the rails on the outside edge, but this will give the hutch an authentic look since this was a common practice among many country cabinetmakers. (2) You can also join the parts with plates or "biscuits." This, however, requires a plate-joining tool.

8

Assemble the case. Dry assemble the case to test the fit of the parts. Place the shelves and the countertop in their respective dadoes, then clamp the upper stiles and the face frame to the sides. If you're satisfied with the fit, take the case apart and reassemble it with glue.

Reinforce the glue joints with square "cut" nails. These are sold at most hardware stores, and are normally used in construction to attach wooden frames to masonry. Used here, they add an antique look to the project. Drill 3/16"-diameter pilot holes for the nails, to prevent them from splitting the wood. Drive the heads flush with the surface of the wood, but don't set them or cover them.

Attach the top with dowels — glue and nails won't keep it in place if the wood starts to cup or bow. Secure the top to the case with band clamps, then drill ⅜"-diameter, 2"-deep stopped holes down through the top and into the sides and upper stiles. Coat the dowels with glue and tap them into the holes so that the ends are flush with the surface of the wood.

Secure the lower end of the upper stiles with dowels, in the same manner you doweled the top to the case. From inside the cabinet, drill holes up through the countertop and into the ends of the stiles. Tap dowels into these holes.

9

Attach the back boards to the case. Attach the back boards to the case with finishing nails. Use the two 3⅛"-wide boards on either side, and alternate the other sizes — 4" and 6" — as shown in the *Back Joinery Detail.* Leave a ¹⁄₁₆" gap between each board, to allow the wood to expand and contract with changes in the weather.

The back boards are *not* glued edge to edge to make a single panel. Wood shrinks and swells ⅛"-¼" *across* the grain for every 12" of width. A solid back panel could move as much as ¾" with changes in temperature and humidity — more movement than the joinery can accommodate. This movement would eventually split the back, pop the case apart, or both.

To solve this problem, country cabinetmakers often cut wide panels into narrow strips, as you have done with the back boards of this hutch. No board is wide enough to move more than ¹⁄₁₆"-⅛". In addition, each board expands and contracts independently of the others. These movements are isolated and will not stress the case joinery.

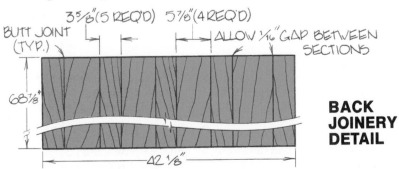

BUTT JOINT (TYP.) 3⅝"(5 REQ'D) 5⅞"(4 REQ'D) ALLOW ¹⁄₁₆" GAP BETWEEN SECTIONS

68⅞"   42⅛"

BACK JOINERY DETAIL

10

Assemble the doors and hinge them to the case. Assemble the door frames with the panels in place. Glue the rails to the stiles, but do *not* glue the panels in place. Let them "float" free in the grooves, so that they can expand and contract. Drill ¼"-diameter dowel holes through the assembled rails and stiles, where shown in the *Left Door Layout* and the *Door Joinery Detail*. Pin the tongues in the grooves with ¼"-diameter pegs.

TRY THIS! Country cabinetmakers often drove square pegs into round holes to make sure that they would stay put. Rip ¼" x ¼" stock for the pegs from some *very* hard wood, such as maple or hickory. Cut this into 1½" lengths. With a knife, whittle off the corners from half the length of each peg to make it partially round. To set the peg, coat it with glue and tap it into a ¼"-diameter hole as far as it will go. Cut the ends off flush with the wood.

Fit the doors in the face frame, planing or sanding away stock as needed. Mortise the door frames and the face frame for the hinges, then mount the doors to the case. The doors in the hutch shown here are "friction fit" and stay shut of their own accord. You may, however, want to use a door catch of some sort. We suggest using bullet catches since these will be least noticeable when you open the doors.

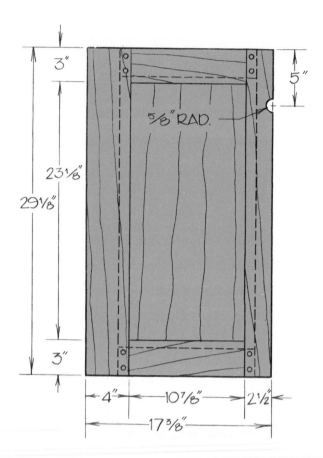

LEFT DOOR LAYOUT

TRY THIS! The doors of this country hutch are hinged to the case with butt hinges, showing that the craftsman who made it spared no expense. Before the Industrial Revolution, the interlocking leaves of a butt hinge were difficult (and expensive) for a blacksmith to make. A country cabinetmaker was more likely to use "rat-tail" hinges — a single leaf wrapped around a pivot. Since there were no knuckles, these were much easier for a blacksmith to make. If you'd rather use rat-tail hinges on your hutch, these are still available from Ball & Ball, 463 W. Lincoln Highway, Exton, PA 19341.

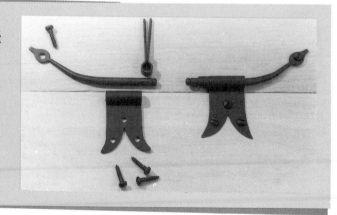

11

Finish the hutch. Remove the doors from the case and the hinges from the doors. Finish sand any parts of the completed hutch that still need it, then apply a finish. We suggest that you use a penetrating finish such as tung oil or Danish oil. Finishes that build up on the surface of the wood will fill in and run in the narrow gaps between the back boards.

If you wish, paint the back boards and the inside of the cabinet a light color — light blue, light green or white. The makers and owners of hutches sometimes did this for two reasons: (1) The plates, glasses, and other kitchenware that they wanted to show off stood out better on the shelves, and (2) the light color made it easier to find items inside the cabinet.

Credits

Contributing Craftsmen and Craftswomen:

> Nick Engler (Knife Caddy, Five-Board Bench, Dry Sink, Spice Chest, Window Shelf, Trestle Table and Benches, Pouting Chair, Candle Sconce)

> Mary Jane Favorite (Porringer Serving Table, Five-Board Bench, Country Village Cutting Boards, Trestle Table and Benches, Pouting Chair, Spice Chest, Candle Sconce)

> John Sweeney (Salt Box/Spoon Rack)

> Stephen Wright (Dough Box)

> Note: Several of the projects in this book were built by country craftsmen whose names have been erased by time. We regret that we cannot tell you who built them; we can only admire their craftsmanship. These pieces include the Pie Safe, Ladder-back Chair, and Hutch.

The designs for the newer projects in this book (those attributed to a designer or builder) are the copyrighted property of the craftsmen and the craftswomen who built them. Readers are encouraged to reproduce these projects for their personal use or for gifts. However, reproduction for sale or profit is forbidden by law.

Special Thanks to:
> Patterson Flowers & Greenhouse, West Milton, Ohio
> Wertz Hardware Stores, West Milton, Ohio
> Robert Menker
> Richard and Susan Burman

Rodale Press, Inc., publishes AMERICAN WOODWORKER™, the magazine for the
serious woodworking hobbyist. For information on how to order your subscription,
write to AMERICAN WOODWORKER™, Emmaus, PA 18098.